HISTORICAL RELICS

OF THE

WHITE MOUNTAINS

D1600123

Entered according to Act of Congress,
in the year 1855, by
J.H. Spaulding
In the Clerk's Office of the District Court
of the District of Masschusetts

Reprint edition Copyright 1998
Second Printing 2004
Bondcliff Books
Library of Congress Catalog Card Number 98-071480
ISBN 0-9657475-3-0

Text layout and design by Tim Leavitt

Printed in the United States by
Sherwin Dodge Printers, Littleton, N.H.

Additional copies of this book may be obtained
directly from:
Bondcliff Books
P.O. Box 385
Littleton, NH 03561

PUBLISHER'S INTRODUCTION

As one of the earliest histories written about the region, John H. Spaulding's ***Historical Relics of the White Mountains*** has long been considered a "classic" in White Mountains literary annals.

The first tidy, leather-bound edition of the book appeared in 1855, and coincided with the surge of interest in the region brought forth, in great part, by the establishment of railroad lines into the White Mountains. Spaulding himself was, at this time, tied keenly to the burgeoning new tourism industry as he served as manager of the two summit hotels atop Mount Washington, the highest peak in the Northeast.

Historical Relics is, in every sense, a combination history and tourism guide. Besides offering an historic glimpse back at the events and people so prominent in the region's settlement, the book also offers in great detail descriptions of many of the natural wonders of the White Mountains—from the barren landscape of Mount Washington and the Presidential Range, to the Old Man of the Mountain in Franconia Notch, and the mysterious Devil's Den in Crawford Notch.

As this book went through several editions in the eight years or so that it remained in print, the author took the liberty to update its contents as time passed on and new events took place in the White Mountains. For instance, early editions of the book did not include the fateful tale of Benjamin Chandler, who perished on Mount Washington in August 1856 after apparently losing his way up the mountain during a summer rain and wind storm. His tragic story only appeared in later editions.

In bringing this book back into print for the first time in more than 130 years, we have taken the liberty to include, for the most part, all material that appeared in the book through its various editions between 1855 and 1862. Any chapters or material that appeared after the first edition are denoted with an asterisk in the Table of Contents page.

Original copies of **Historical Relics** are still available to book collectors in this day and age, but their rarity has driven up the price to levels no longer affordable to the average reader. It is with this fact in mind that we are proud to put John H. Spaulding's **Historical Relics of the White Mountains** back into readers' hands again.

ABOUT THE AUTHOR

John Hubbard Spaulding was a North Country native, born August 17, 1821, and raised in the Connecticut River town of Lancaster, just a few miles west of Mount Washington and the Presidential Range. His grandfather, Edward Spaulding, was one of Lancaster's first settlers.

According to previously published accounts of his life, John Spaulding was barely three years old when both his father (John Wilson Spaulding) and his mother (Electa Stebbins Spaulding) died. He was adopted by his uncle and aunt (William and Sarah Spaulding) and raised to adulthood by them on their Lancaster farm.

After spending his early adult years as a successful school teacher, he gradually learned the practice of land surveying and was eventually hired by the government to serve on the survey team which established the permanent boundary between the northern New England states of Maine, New Hampshire and Vermont and neighboring Canada following the signing of the Webster and Ashburton Treaty in 1842.

Over a two-year span in the late 1840s, Spaulding purchased several hundred acres of prime timber land in and around Lancaster and established two sawmills for the manufacturing of lumber. During this same time period, he married Emilene Courser of Guildhall, Vt., with whom he would have two children, John H. Jr. and Debby Ann.

One year after the first mountaintop hotel (the Summit House) was constructed on Mount Washington in 1852 by Joseph Hall and Lucius Rosebrook, another of John Spaulding's uncles, Samuel Fitch Spaulding, along with two Jefferson businessman (Abraham Bedell and Anson Stillings), built the stone Tip-Top House. John Spaulding, who was also a partner in the venture, served as manager of the hotel once it opened in late July of 1853. The next year, after the Spauldings acquired an interest in the Summit House, John Spaulding was named chief manager of both hotels and continued to serve in that capacity for some nine years.

It was during his third year as manager of the summit hotels that *Historical Relics of the White Mountains* first appeared in print in 1855. Over the course of the next eight years, it was reissued in various forms and editions. When the Spauldings relinquished ownership of the two hotels in 1859, one source indicates Spaulding's copyright to the book was included in the sale.

JOHN H. SPAULDING

John Spaulding's legendary link to Mount Washington was further solidified in February 1862 when he and two companions, Franklin White and Chapin Brooks, became the first people to stay atop the mountain in the dead of winter. The trio lodged themselves in the vacant Summit House for two uncomfortable days and nights after a midwinter storm enveloped the mountain. Spaulding Lake, a spectacular half-acre tarn on the floor of the Great Gulf between Mount Washington and Northern Presidentials, also bears the author's name. He visited the tiny lake in 1853, applying his own family name to the then nameless tarn.

After leaving Mount Washington and the mountain hotel business, Spaulding moved to Rosendale, New York in 1865, and was hired on as superintendent of the Lawrenceville Cement Company. He stayed with this firm for more than a quarter century, then returned to the White Mountains region in the late 1880s. His last visit to Mount Washington's summit reportedly took place in 1891, when the then 70-year-old Spaulding hiked to the mountaintop. Two years later, on his 72nd birthday, he died in Whitefield, N.H.

Mike Dickerman,
April 1998

INTRODUCTION

There may be no locality combining more general interest for the pleasure-seeking tourist than the White Mountains. Here every season thousands come from different climes, on a pilgrimage, that they may pay most worshipful tribute in spirit-felt wonder, and songs of praise. My apology for attempting to originate and compile the following pages, is the belief that the curiosity of the travelling public requires a work embodying my design. The pencil of "Oakes" and pen of "Becket" have nicely defined every explored locality, interestingly connected with the particular geography of these mountains; besides which, the number of those may be called *"legion"* who have made fancied famous record for the world of their White Mountain impressions. These mountains are a fadeless pictured page in Nature's wonderful book,— or a gigantic monument of ruins formed by an overwhelming change, that widely disfigured the original geological formation of this wild region; and as a massive rock-shadow in a strange land, is to a journey-sick pilgrim with a gushing cold-water spring by his feet, so my impressions of these famous *"old peaks"* now rise to my sight. An ambitious presence in fancy is with me now, with a voice saying, like a prophetic whisper from *"Gheistland,"* *"Rescue from* the twilight of forgetfulness the Historical Relics of the White Mountains!" The *curious data* of olden times—the *antiquities* of this anciently named Agiochook, with the statistical facts of modern origin, necessary for a concise history of *"these bald old heads of nature"*—have never been tangibly combined. The trials and daring exploits of the fearless adventurers, who in other days filled the historic blank of this renowned locality, are rich with rarities for a work of interest to the reading world. Their life-relics have twined around them, by traditionary remembrance, pleasant associations of undecayable interest. We may for future visions gaze back from the cloud-capped crags into the valley of the past, and rescue from the oblivious mist of years the oral monuments, that, tinctured by the life-passion of times long gone, linger like visions of light upon the map of memory.

Vanity is not the power that prompts me to desire success in this task; but as storm and time cover the names chiselled upon the top crag of Mount Washington with moss, so, with a round of years, "Old Morality" *should come,* to brighten up the vestiges of the past, and catalogue new events with the re-chiselled.

The antiquarian collections of interesting facts, found in the library of the Massachusetts Historical Society, having been open to my inquiry, my humble tribute of respect is due that society for the arrangement by which my research has been favored; and their assistant librarian, John Appleton, M.D., is, for his politeness to me as a stranger, deserving my lasting gratitude. The kindness of J.M. Rix, Esq., of Lancaster, in giving me free access to his library of choice books, is happily remembered. N. Noyes, Esq., of Boston, and B.F. Whidden, Esq., of Lancaster, have my sincere thanks for assisting me in obtaining the facts here registered, from the most authentic records. J.H.S.

Lancaster, June 1855.

TABLE OF CONTENTS

HISTORICAL RELICS

OF

THE WHITE MOUNTAINS

LEGENDARY ORIGIN OF THE WHITE MOUNTAINS

COLD storms were in the northern wilderness, and a lone red hunter wandered without food, chilled by the frozen wind. He lost his strength, and could find no game; and the dark cloud that covered his life-path made him weary of wandering. He fell down upon the snow, and a dream carried him to a wide, happy valley, filled with musical streams, where singing birds and game were plenty. His spirit cried aloud for joy; and the *"Great Master of Life"* waked him from his sleep, gave him a dry coal and a flint-pointed spear, telling him that by the shore of the lake he might live, and find fish with his spear, and fire from his dry coal. One night, when he had laid down his coal, and seen a warm fire spring up therefrom, with a blinding smoke, a loud voice came out of the flame, and a great noise, like thunder, filled the air; and there rose up a vast pile of broken

rocks. Out of the cloud resting upon the top came numerous streams, dancing down, foaming cold; and the
voice spake to the astonished red hunter, saying, *"Here
the Great Spirit will dwell, and watch over his favorite
children." - Old Legend.*

FIRST VISIT, IN 1631

DR. BELKNAP, the learned historian of New Hampshire, gives Walter Neal the credit of being the first
explorer of these mountains, as early as the year 1632.
Morrill's N. H. Gazetteer of 1817 concludes, from the
best authorities, that Robert Neal, Walter Neal and others, visited these mountains as early as the year 1631.
Josselyn, in his New England Rarities, gives the following description, which, with little variation, is found
also in Belknap, as an extract from Hubbard's MS.
History, credited to Walter Neal:

"Four score miles (upon a direct line) to the N.W. of
Scarboro' a ridge of mountains runs N.W. and N.E. an
hundred leagues, known by the name of White Hills,
upon which lieth snow all the year, and is a landmark
twenty miles off the sea. It is a rising ground from the
sea-shore to these hills, and they are inaccessible but
by the gullys which the dissolved snow hath made. In
these gulleys grow savin bushes, which, being taken
hold of, are a good help to the climbing discoverer.
Upon the top of the highest of these mountains is a

large level, or plain, of a day's journey over, whereon nothing grows but moss. At the further end of this plain is another hill, called the *'Sugarloaf,'* to outward appearance a rude heap of massive stones, piled one upon another; and you may, as you ascend, step from one stone to another, as if you were going up a pair of stairs, but winding still about the hill, till you come to the top, which will require half a day's time, and yet it is not above a mile, where there is also a level of about an acre of ground, with a pond of clear water in the midst of it, which you may hear run down; but how it ascends is a mystery. From this rocky hill you may see the whole country around about. It is far above the lower clouds, and from hence we beheld vapor (like a great pillar) drawn up by the sunbeams out of a great lake, or pond, into the air, where it was formed into a cloud. The country beyond these hills, northward, is daunting terrible, being full of rocky hills, as thick as moll-hills in a meadow, and clothed with infinite thick woods."*— *N.E. Rarities, 3-4.*

---

* Another writer, after giving a similar description, adds, "We had great expectation of finding precious stones on these mountains;" and something resembling crystals being picked up, was sufficient to give them the name of "Crystal Hills." They were long called by that name.—AUTHOR.

DARBY FIELD'S VISIT, IN 1642.

June 4th, 1642.—"Darby Field" (says Winthrop, in his Journal), "an Irishman living about Piscat, being accompanied with two Indians, went to the top of the White Hill. He made his journey in eighteen days. His relation, at his return, was, that it was about 160 miles from Saco; that after 40 miles travel he did, for the most part, ascend; and within 12 miles of the top was neither tree nor grass, but low savins, which they went upon the top of, sometimes; but a continual ascent upon rocks, on a ridge, between two valleys, filled with snow, out of which came two branches of the Saco river, which met at the foot of the hill, where was an Indian town, of some 200 people. Some of them accompanied him within 8 miles of the top, but durst go no further, telling him that no Indian ever dared to go higher, and that he would die if he went. So they staid there till his return, and *his* two Indians took courage by his example, and went with him. They went divers times through thick clouds, for a good space; and within 4 miles of the top they had no clouds, but very cold. By the way among the rocks there was two ponds: one a blackish water, and the other reddish. The top of all was plain, about 60 ft. square. On the north side was such a precipice as they could scarcely discern the bottom. They had neither cloud nor wind on the top, and moderate heat. All the country above him seemed a level, except here and there a hill rising above the rest, and far beneath them. He saw, to the north, a great water, which he judged to be 100 miles broad, but could see no land beyond it. The sea by Saco seemed as if it had been within 20 miles. He saw, also, a sea to the eastward, which he judged to be the gulf of Canada. He saw some great waters in parts to the westward, which he judged to be the great lake Canada river (St. Lawrence) came out of. He found there much Muscovy glass; they could rive out pieces 40 ft. long, and 7 or 8 broad. When he came back to the Indians, he found them drying themselves by the fire; for they had a great tempest of wind and rain. About a month after, he went again, with five or six of his company. Then they had some wind on the top, and some clouds above them, which hid the sun. They brought some stones, which they supposed has been diamonds; but they were most crystals."* —*Winthrop's Journal,* p. 247.

INDIAN VENERATION FOR AGIOCHOOK.

According to antiquarian research, the aboriginal name of the White Mountains was "Agiochook;" spelt, also Agiocochook, Agicoochooke, Agiochooke; signifying, by ancient Indian nomenclature, *"Mountain of the Snowy Forehead, and Home of the Great Spirit."* Schoolcraft, in his "Indian Wigwam," page 248, gives, as the Algonquin pronunciation of these mountains,

---

* We may reasonably conclude that Darby Field's trail was up the ridge between Tuckerman's Ravine and the valley of Dry River.—AUTHOR.

"Waubik," or "Waumbick;" meaning *"White Rock."*
Becket, in his "Guide," calls them, from ancient au-
thority, "Waumbeket Methna," signifying mountains of
the *"Snowy Foreheads."* The lore of legend, the voice
of tradition, and the record of history, point to these
mountains as a locality of great interest. In olden times,
from far and near have come the brave and fair red
children of the wilderness, to offer, in wild, shadowy
glens, their sacrifices of vengeance and love; and where
their songs rose, with the echoes of thundering waterfalls, to mingle with the roaring wind of the tempest
cloud, upon the snow-covered rock, there they rever-
ently believed the Great Spirit listened with satisfaction to their tributes of esteem. When the first white
man came here, to climb to the top of this bald mountain, an old Indian, with his tomahawk of stone, flint-
pointed arrow, and tanned war-dress, from the skins of
moose and bear, standing proudly erect, shook his head,
and said, "The Great Spirit dwells there; he covers steps
above the green leaves with the darkness of the fire
tempest. No foot-marks are seen returning from his
home in the clouds."

The explorer's thirst for daring adventure overruled
the fear created by the Indians' superstition; and, after
learning that the Great Spirit sent a high wind, in a thick
mist, and caught up to the top of Agiochook a single
sanop and his squaw, that the wilderness and all the

mountains except this, might be covered for two suns with water, and that they might then return as the only mortals who should ever come down the "White Rock" from his dwelling place, he went to the top, and safely returned. All old authentic records agree, that the aborigines unitedly had a peculiar superstitious veneration for these mountains. They considered them the dwelling-place of the invisible One, who, with a motion of his hand, could raise a storm; and accordingly they deemed it pardonless sacrilege to ascend them. Traditions teach us that a few have been found so daring (in the long history of the Indians) as to press, with their moccasined feet the moss that grows above the region of scrub vegetation; and such have been doomed to wander forever invisibly among wild gorges, with no resting-place save the damp, cold caverns in the rocks, and no hope of ever reaching the *"happy land,"* beyond the setting sun. To this day, those are to be found who credulously believe that the strange noises often heard among the shadowy cliffs (instead of giving credit to wolves and wild-cats) proceed from lost spirits, that miserably exist here in hopeless torment, perpetually bewailing their fate.

GEOGRAPHICAL SITUATION OF WHITE MOUNTAINS.

These mountains are situated in the State of New Hampshire, County of Coos. Their latitude is 44° 16' 34$\frac{1}{2}$" north, and longitude 77° 20' west. Since their discovery by the early voyagers along the wild coast of New England, they have ever been regarded with wonder and admiration. Deep, shadowy gorges, where the everlasting waterfall lives among massy crags, with its endless thunder-song; the yawning chasms, filled with snow, and romantic, flowery glens, shaded by a gnarled growth of old forest-trees, combined with an area of fifty thousand three hundred and forty-one acres of shattered rocks, piled high up to the clouds, in the wildest disorder imaginable, form the remarkable outline of this famous locality. No wonder that the rude, nature-tanned son of the wilderness, as he gazed upon this gigantic pile of rocks, standing up from its original bed six thousand two hundred and eight-five feet into the clouds, was filled with superstitious veneration; for here; in all coming time, the enlightened sons of science may pay willing homage, where the Great Spirit dwelt in storms, and gave the thunder his voice, and the lightning the flash of his anger!

GEOLOGICAL FEATURES.

According to the report of the geological surveyor of the State of New Hampshire, Dr. C.T. Jackson, the features of these mountains, geologically considered, possess little peculiar interest. The rocks in places consist of a coarse variety of mica slate, passing into gneiss, and containing a few crystals of black tourmaline, and quartz. The cone of Mount Washington and its summit are covered with myriads of angular and flat blocks, and slabs of mica slate, piled in confusion one upon another. These are identical in nature with the rocks in place, and leave no marks of transportation or abrasion by the action of water. The nucleus of these mountains is granite rock, and the mica slate found on the top of the different peaks is but a superficial crust; and it is observable that the sedimentary deposit, or granite, has been disturbed by upheavals, which, with the action of a comparatively moderate heat for ages, has doubled back and twisted and broken these large sheet of mica slate, and left the fragments exposed in the wildest confusion, for mortal wonder.

MINERALS.

Various local traditions are in existence to prove the adventurous belief of many, that yet, in some unexplored or enchantment-guarded places, are mines of wealth of immense value. These tend to tantalize the imagination of many; with how much probability for future realization is not my province to decide. In this book will be found certain of these traditions, which, in their proper places are deemed worthy of record, for gratification of public curiosity.

The minerals yet obtained among these mountains are not satisfactory to the spirit of discovery. Southerly from the top of Mount Washington is found a vein of quartz, containing crystals of fluor-spar of apple-green color, and crystallized in its primary form. This attracts the attention of collectors of minerals, and is worthy of notice as a curiosity. A few quartz crystals, in the form of six-sided prisms, also occur at the same place. Near the location of these crystals has been found, lately, a new bed of black tourmaline, which has furnished some finely-shaped crystals. These specimens are found in large masses of milk-quartz, near the route to the summit of the mountain, from the old Crawford or Davis path. On a branch of Dry River, have been found some remarkably large and transparent specimens of quartz crystallization, and much search has been made there for a bed of diamonds that are of a rare quality. An old hunter (Sanborn) is now living, who faithfully affirms that, many years ago, while fishing, up a small branch of Dry river, under the eastern side of Mount Pleasant, he came to a place where the water ran between two high white rocks so covered with perfect diamonds that it was blinding to his eyes to look upon the same. He succeeded in breaking off three with his fish-pole, which he sold for five dollars each, at Old Abel Crawford's. Several exploring parties have been in search of this treasure; and as lately as 1853 the same old gray-headed hunter who made the discovery, went with two other treasure-seekers, armed with drills and power, &c., and made thorough search, for several days, among all the small northern branches of this river. Not far from the top of Mount Washington, in every direction from that point, are found veins of white and rose-colored quartz, with here and there fine crystals of quartz; and on Mount Franklin have been found many fine specimens of crystallization. In or near the gateway of the Notch are found rare amethystine crystals, specimens of which will readily sell to mineralogists for five dollars each. Tin is found in veins on some of the southern spurs of these mountains; in the valley of Dry River, are streams so impregnated with iron that the bushes and trees along their shores are loaded with red rust; and in such places not a fish, or thing of animal life, can be found. Particles of lead, with specks of silver, are found on a branch of Peabody river; but so far nothing of that kind has been found sufficient for important notice. As yet, there are many deep glens and wild crags in all this mighty pile of mountains, where the explorer has never left the print of his feet upon the moss. Without doubt more minerals will be found before these mountains are perfectly well known.

SCIENTIFIC MEASUREMENTS OF THE MOUNTAINS.

Rev. D. Cutler twice visited the Crystal Hills, in the beginning of the eighteenth century, and took barometrical observations, by which he calculates the highest peak to be ten thousand feet above the sea.

Dr. Belknap, in his famous New Hampshire History,

is persuaded by his observations, that the computation of ten thousand feet as the height of the Crystal Hills is too moderate, and he concludes that subsequent calculations will make them much higher. Mr. Bowditch published, in the transactions of the American Academy, a logarithmic calculation, founded on Professor Peck's barometrical observations, giving the Crystal Hills an elevation of seven thousand and fifty-five feet. Capt. Partridge, United States engineer, visited these mountains in 1804, and took barometrical observations on several of the principal peaks. His calculations give to the highest summit an elevation of six thousand one hundred and three feet.

July 2d, 1816, a mountain barometer of Englefield's construction stood, on the highest peak, at noon, 24.23, the accompanying thermometer being at 57. Same day, at Cambridge, Mass., similar observations were taken; and a logarithmic calculation, made by Professor Farrar, from the data thus obtained, resulted in establishing six thousand two hundred and twenty-five feet above the waters of the ocean as the height of Mount Washington. A geometrical admeasurement taken by Professor Shuttuck, on the north-west side of the mountain, on a plain near the present ruins of the Fabyan Stand, gave to the summit an elevation of six thousand two hundred and sixty-eight feet. In 1840, C.T. Jackson, geological surveyor of New Hampshire, by means of barometrical and thermometrical observations, made for a period of twelve hours, at a time when the weather was remarkably favorable, and the atmospheric pressure was stationary throughout the state, as shown by other observations made at the same time, ascertained the height of Mount Washington to be six thousand two hundred and twenty-six feet above high-water mark at Portsmouth. According to the *Cincinnati Times* of Dec. 1st, 1853, the United States coast surveyors, in Aug., 1853, made, by calculation, the summit of Mount Washington six thousand seven hundred and forty-three feet above the sea. William A. Goodwin, Esq., one of the engineers of the Atlantic and St. Lawrence rail road, by a survey made by levelling from the ocean to the top of Mount Washington, makes the height of that peak six thousand two hundred and eighty-five feet. Professor Guyot, of Cambridge, Mass., by barometrical observations taken at the same time, nearly agrees with Mr. Goodwin's survey. This is, doubtless, the actual height of Mount Washington. In 1854, Messrs. Ricker and Cavis, chief engineers of the White Mountain carriage-road, by actual survey, made the height six thousand two hundred and eighty-four feet.

HEIGHT OF WHITE MOUNTAINS.

Mt. Washington,	6,285 ft.	Mt. Monroe,	5,349 ft.
" Adams,	5,790 "	" Franklin,	4,850 "
" Jefferson,	5,710 "	" Pleasant,	4,715 "
" Madison,	5,361 "	" Clinton,	4,200 "
" Clay,	5,011 "		

PERPETUAL CONGELATON.

Many suppose that in the darkest and most shadowy gorges of these mountains snow and ice may be found at any season of the year. This is a mistaken opinion; for it can be satisfactorily proved, by those who know, that the latest appearance of old snow, for several years past, has been in Tuckerman's Ravine, as late as Aug. 20th. This ravine, by observation, is found to retain its winter burden the longest; and being, as it is, fairly exposed to the sun, this, unexplained, appears remarkable. The northern winds of our extremely cold winters pile there, from the surrounding summits, a good share of the snow that falls on them; and there is but little doubt that in our most severe seasons for wintry storms, the snow-drift in this wild gorge is a hundred feet deep. Much has been written and said about the endless *snow-arch* and perpetual snow-bank of Tuckerman's Ravine, by those, even, who, with the light of science around them, should be aware that in the latitude of these mountains the line of perpetual congelation is, by scientific observation, found to be at an elevation of seven thousand eight hundred and seventy-two feet above the sea level. To strengthen the conclusion that the snow may here be seen in piles a hundred feet deep, the following true account may here be noticed:

DINING UNDER FORTY FEET OF SNOW.

The water that runs from Tuckerman's Ravine passes under the great snow-bank, and, with the warmth of summer, wears a curious channel. July 16th, 1854, D.O. Macomber, president of the Mount Washington carriage-road, and Engineer C.H.V. Cavis, of that road, with the author of these pages, dined in that snow arch. It was then two hundred and sixty-six feet long, eighty-four feet wide, and forty feet high, by measurement, to the snow roof, from which constantly dripped down cold icewater around us. A heavy thunder-shower, while there, passed over us, and after the shower we found any quantity of little hardy *alpine flowers,* fresh and fair, watered by the water from the great bank.

THE VETERAN PILOT

In 1792, near the famous "Giant's Grave,"* lived a solitary pioneer of this mountain wilderness; and a rude cabin of logs, covered with bark, was his only shelter.

* A well-known mound near the Fabyans ruins by the northern shore of the Amonoosuc.

This man had no neighbor nearer than twelve miles, and naught but a rough hunting-path, marked by spotted trees, led thither through the notch. Wild beasts were plenty in all this mountain region. The first glowing accounts of the early hunters scarcely equalled the reality. All the streams were full of trouts. Moose, bears, wolves and wild-cats, were all very numerous in their undisturbed haunts, within the shadow of these towering crags, where the Indian hunters dared not leave his foot-marks. The name of this white man, who here lived in solitude, was Abel Crawford—the one who in after years most justly gained the title of the *Veteran Pilot*. He was the *first guide* for gentlemen strangers, who first came here to see the mountain scenery, independent of any scientific purpose. Let *the name Crawford* live with this mountain memory! The steps of the old *Veteran Pilot* were among those gray old cliffs, and dark, shadowy gorges, when log-cabins were the only habitation in all this northern wilderness. Then he dressed in the tanned skins of the moose, and became in the chase a perfect Nimrod and a true disciple of the famed Izaak Walton.

FIRST HOTEL

By the present ruins of the old Fabyan stand, on the westerly end of the "Giant's Grave," was erected the first public house for White Mountain visitors, in the year 1803. A record of this is found in E.A. Crawford's journal, page twenty, of which the following is a true extract: "My grandfather built a large and convenient two-story dwelling on an elevated spot (this elevation has since been named Giant's Grave). This house had two stories under ground. From the chamber over this, in the second story, was an outside door, which opened so that one could walk out on this fine hill, from which, to the stranger, the view was beautiful."

When owned by E.A. Crawford, in the year 1819, that house was burned; and it is a singular fact that this is the only fine locality for a public (White Mountain) house, in full view from the tip-top rock of Mount Washington; and yet here three public houses have been burned since the year 1805, on and near this "Giant's Grave."

INDIAN PROPHECY ON GIANT'S GRAVE.

There is a strange tradition extant, of an Indian, who, long years ago, stood on that mount, with a blazing pitch pine torch, lighted at a tree struck by lightning, and, swinging it wildly around in the darkness, he said, *"No pale-face shall take deep root here; this the Great Spirit whispered in my ear."*

THE WHITE MOUNTAIN GIANT.

The name of E.A. Crawford is deeply chiselled upon the rocks of this granite Mount built by nature (Mount Washington); and the lady who shared in life his joys and sorrows has, in her "White Mountain History," reared a testimonial to his memory. Will not my humble tribute of a stone, laid in silence upon his grave, be accepted by all who pleasantly cherish the remembrance of *"Ethan of the Hills,"* or the *"White Mountain Giant"?*

The subject of this sketch was born in Guildhall, Vermont, in the year 1792. When but a mere lad his parents moved to the White Mountains, and here he grew up a giant mountaineer, illustrating by his hardy habits, how daring enterprise and pure mountain climate nerve the man and stamp the *hero* upon mortality. Inheriting the house on the westerly end of the "Giant's Grave," with an encumbrance that made him worse than destitute of all worldly goods, he was one day shocked, when returning from hunting on the hills, to see his home burned down, and his wife and infant sheltered only by an open shed. Twelve miles one way, and six the other, to neighbors, here he was with his little family in the wilderness, destitute of every comfort, save that of hope. The sunshine of joy, unclouded by sorrow, and the warm smiles of good fortune, seem ever attendant upon the lives of some, constantly beckoning their favorites forward to the green fields of abundance, and bowers of pleasure and ease. Others, perchance born under a less favoring star, in their growth rise up like giants, breasting manfully, step by step, the wrecking storms of adversity, and by their own heroic exertions, hew out for themselves characters deeply lined, amid the black shadows of sorrow and disappointment. Of such a mould was the spirit of Ethan A. Crawford. The inconveniences of poverty, that come like a strong man armed upon poor mortality, and sickness and the many hardships linked with every-day life in a new settlement, fell to this man's share. Yet he cheerfully performed the duties of life with an iron resolution, that stood misfortune's shocks as firmly as his own mountains stand storms and the changes of time. He was a tall, finely-proportioned man; and, though called by many the "White Mountain Giant," beneath the rough exterior of the hardy mountaineer glowed constantly, in a heroic heart, the warm fire of love and manly virtue. The artless prattle of his little children was sweet music to his spirit, and his ambitious aspirations were constantly invigorated by social comfort with his little family.

CARRYING THE KETTLE AND DEER.

The first display of Ethan's *giant strength* recorded is of his carrying on his head, across the Amonoosuc river, a potash-kettle, weighing four hundred pounds.

In 1821 he caught a full-grown deer, in a wild gorge, four miles from his home; and as the trap had not broken his leg, and he appeared quite gentle, he thought to lead him home. Failing in his attempt to do this, he shouldered him and trudged homeward, over hill and through tangled brushwood, feeling by the way, perchance, like Crusoe, with his lamas, how fine it would be to have a park and many deer to show his visitors. But his day-visions vanished; for, on arriving home, he found the deer so much injured that he died.

Another time, he *caught a wild mountain-buck* in a snare; and, finding him too heavy to shoulder, he made him a halter of withes, and succeeded in halter-leading him so completely, that, after nearly a day spent in the attempt, he arrived at home with his prize, much to the wonder of all.

THE GIANT LUGGING THE OLD BEAR.

In 1829 Ethan caught a good-sized bear in a trap; and thought to bind him with withes, and lead him home as he had the buck. In attempting to do this, the bear would catch with his paws at the trees; and our hero, not willing to be outwitted by a bear, managed to get him on his shoulder, and, with one hand firmly hold of his nose, carried him two miles homeward. The bear, not well satisfied with his prospects, entered into a serious engagement with his captor, and by scratching and biting succeeded in tearing off his vest and one pantaloon-leg, so that Ethan laid him down so hard upon the rocks that he died. That fall he caught ten bears in that same wild glen.

The first bear kept in the White Mountains for a show

was caught by Ethan, while returning from the Mountain with two young gentlemen he had been up with as guide. Seeing a small bear cross their path, they followed him to a tree, which he climbed. Ethan climbed after, and, succeeding in getting him, tied his mouth up with a handkerchief, and backed him home. This bear he provided with a trough of water, a strap and pole; and here he was for a long time kept, as the first tame bear of the mountains. This was about the 1829.

Ethan caught a wild-cat with a birch withe! Once, when passing down the Notch, he was attracted to a tree by the barking of his dog, where, up among the thick branches, he discovered a full-grown wild-cat. Having only a small hatchet with him, he cut two long birch withes, and, twisting them well together, made a slip-noose, which he run up through the thick leaves; and while the cat was watching the dog, he managed to get this noose over his head, and, with a sudden jerk, brought him to the ground. His dog instantly seized him, but was willing to beat a retreat till reinforced by his master, who with a heavy club came to the rescue. The skin of this cat, when stretched, measured over six feet.

Ethan's *two close shots* are worthy of note. One fall, while setting a sable line, about two miles back of the Notch, he discovered a little lake, set, like a diamond, in a rough frame-work of beetling crags. The fresh

signs of moose near, and trouts seen in its shining waters, was sufficient inducement to spend a night by its
shady shore. About sunset, while engaged in catching
a string of trouts, his attention was suddenly arrested
by a loud splashing in the still water around a rocky
point, where, on looking, he saw two large brown moose
pulling up lily-roots, and fighting the flies. Prepared
with an extra charge, he fired; and before the first report died in echoes among the peaks, the second followed, and both moose fell dead in the lake. Ethan
labored hard to drag his game ashore; but late that
evening bright visions of marrow-bones and broiled
trouts flitted like realities around him. That night a
doleful dirge rose in that wild gorge; but our hero slept
soundly, between two warm moose-skins. He cared
not for the wild wolves that scented the taint of the
fresh blood in the wind. That little mountain sheet is
now, from the above circumstance, known as *"Ethan's
Pond."*

Ethan was always proud to speak of how he *carried
a lady two miles down the mountain on his shoulders.*
It was no uncommon affair for him to shoulder a man
and lug him down the mountain; but his more delicate
attempts to pack a young lady down the steep rocks, he
seemed to regard as an important incident in his adventurous career. Miss E. Woodward was the name of
the lady who received from the Mountain Giant such

marked attention. By a wrong step she became very lame, and placing, as well as he could, a cushion of coats upon his right shoulder, the lady became well seated, and he thus brought her down to where they left their horses.

By Adino N. Brackett's Journal, published in Moore's His. Col., vol. 1st, page 97, it appears that Adino N. Brackett, John W. Weeks, Gen. John Willson, Charles J. Stuart, Esq., Noyes S. Dennison, and Samuel A. Pearson, Esq., from Lancaster, N.H., with Philip Carrigan and E. A. Crawford, went up, July 31st, 1820, to name the different summits. Gen. John Willson, of Boston, is now, 1855, the only survivor of that party. "They made Ethan their pilot, and loaded him with provisions and blankets, like a pack-horse; and then, as they began to ascent, they piled on top of this load their coats." This party had a fine time; and, after giving names of our sages to the different peaks, according to their altitude, they drank health to these hoary cliffs, in honor to the illustrious men whose names they were, from this date, to bear; then, *curled down among the rocks,* without fire, on the highest crag, they doubtless spent the first night mortals ever spent on that elevated place. In the morning, after seeing the sun rise out of the ocean far, far below them, they descended westerly from the apex about a mile, and came to a beautiful sheet of water (Lake of the Clouds), near a ridge of

rocks, which, when they left, they named *"Blue Pond."*
It doubtless looked blue to them; for something they
carried in bottles so weakened the limbs of one of the
party that Ethan was, from this place, burdened with a
back-load of mortality, weighing two hundred pounds,
down to the Amonoosuc valley. Thus we find Ethan
most emphatically the *"Giant of the Mountains."* He
never hesitated to encounter any danger that appeared
in his path, whether from wild beasts, flood, or mountain tempest.

The *First Bridle-path* on the White Mountains was
made in 1819. As there had got to be ten or twelve
visitors a year, to see these mountains, at this date, Ethan
thought, to accommodate his company, he would cut a
path as far as the region to scrub vegetation extended.
It had been very difficult to go without a road, clam-
bering over trees, up steep ledges, through streams, and
over the hedgy scrub-growth; and accordingly, when
the act of a path being made was published, the fame
of this region spread like wild-fire. This path was
started at the head of the notch near Gibb's House, and,
extending to the top of Mount Clinton, reached from
thence to the top of Mount Washington, nearly where
Gibb's Path now is. Soon after the completion of this
path, the necessity of a cabin, where visitors could stop
through the night, was perceivable by Ethan; and accordingly be built *a stone cabin,* near the top of Mount

Washington, by a spring of water that lives there, and spread in it an abundance of soft moss for beds, that those who wished to stop here through the night, to see the sun set and rise, might be accommodated. This rude home for the traveller was soon improved, and furnished with a small stove, an iron chest, and a long roll of sheet-lead;—the chest was to secure from the bears and hedge-hogs the camping-blankets; and, according to tradition, around that old chest many who hungered have enjoyed a hearty repast. That roll of lead was for visitors to engrave their names on with a sharp iron. Alas! *that* tale-telling old chest was buried by an avalanche. How all things pass away!

In 1821 the *first ladies* visited Mount Washington. This party, of which these ladies numbered three, had Ethan for its guide, and, proceeding to the stone cabin, waited there through a storm for several days, that they might be the first females to accomplish the unrecorded feat of ascending Mount Washington. This heroic little party was the Misses Austin, of Portsmouth, N.H., being accompanied by their brother and an Esq. Stuart, of Lancaster. Everything was managed as much for their comfort as possible; the little stone cabin was provided with an outside addition, in which the gentlemen staid, that their companions might be more retired and comfortable. This party came near being what the sailor might call "weather-bound." They were obliged to send back for more provisions; and at last the severe mountain-storm passed away, and that for which they had ambitiously endured so much exposure was granted them. They went to the top, had a fine prospect, and, after an absence of five days, returned from the mountains, in fine spirits, highly gratified with their adventure. This heroic act should confer an honor upon the names of this pioneer party, as everything was managed with so much prudence and modesty that there was not left even a shadow for reproach, save by those who felt themselves outdone; so says record.

In the summer of 1840 the first horse that ever climbed the rocks of Mount Washington was rode up by old Abel Crawford. The old man was then seventy-five years old, and, though his head was whitened by the snows of many winters, his blood was stirred, on that occasion, by the ambitious animation of more youthful days. There he sat proudly upon his noble horse, with uncovered head, and the wind played lightly with his venerable white locks. Truly that was a picture worthy an artist's skill. Holding that horse by the rein, there stood his son Ethan, as guide to his old father. The son and the parent!—worthy representatives of the mighty monument, to the remembrance of which, their pioneer exertions have added fadeless fame. From that day a new era dawned on these mountains. Forget not the veteran Abel, and Ethan *"the White Mountain Giant."*

The White Mountain Guides should all be remembered. In our lengthy notice of Ethan, *the White Mountain Giant,* we do not mean to eclipse the worthy deeds of other noble mountain spirits, who have followed his old path, and even made new ones for their own feet. This mountain region is truly haunted, as it were, by peculiar influences, that call to its attractions as dauntless men for guides as our New England mountain-land can boast. Ethan A. Crawford came here when this was a wilderness-land, unknown to fame. The fashionable world knew nothing of its peculiarities. He spent much time, even the energies of his life, exploring the wild gorges and dangerous peaks of the mountains, and became a mighty hunter. He was, in fact, the bold pioneer who, with his old father, opened the way whereby the "Crystal Hills" became known to the world. "Honor to whom honor is due!" Then let us not be unmindful of Ethan, who grappled with nature in her wildness, and made gigantic difficulties surmountable; and let us remember the names of "Tom Crawford," "Hartford," Hall," "Cogswell;" "Dana, and Lucius M. Rosebrook," "Leavitt," "Hayes," and others, who have followed piloting for a series of years on these mountains. These are all men whose hands the tourist was comparatively safe; and, though the most of the above names are with the past, others are on the stage, who have an ambitious desire to outdo, even, in skill and management, those whose footsteps they follow. We will not praise the living guides of the White Mountains; their actions speak monuments of honor to their own names. Have confidence in their integrity; and may they never betray their trust!

TRADITIONS OF SILVER AND GOLD

From an ancient record, in manuscript, found in an old, worm-eaten chest, among files of papers relating to the early exploration and survey of the northern wilderness, appears the following:

"Espying what could be found in this wild country, as we came to the shadow of this exceeding great mountain, we drew near to a little lake among high rocks. Here we still hunted a moose, and, kindling a fire of pine knots, enjoyed a great feast. Game was thick here; and we could as easily count the sand as the spotted fish in the stream. By this water we discovered a pine log, much decayed, with fire-marks on the ends, and the middle was burned out like as if a fire had been kindled on it to make it a rude canoe. We found good store of curious stones, that we esteemed to be diamonds (crystal quartz). At the foot of a high rock, near the water, we picked up certain leaves of fine silver and gold as thick as a man's nail; and we found all the little mountain streams shining with particles of silver, with many shining bits in the rocks. After many days of toilsome travel, we returned from this wonderful mountain, with bloody, bare feet, and got of the Indians moccasins, made of raw moose-hide. We found rude wigwams, made of poles stuck in the ground, with birch-bark spread over. Around these hunting places were many horns of moose, and piles of bones, eagle-claws and bear-skins, which made us liken these great valleys among the hills to the home of many wild beasts. No man, among all the wild men we met, dared go up to the high, naked rock, for fear the *'Great Master of Life'* would destroy them. In a black storm of rain that fell there, the mountain trembled, and the rocks were like altars burning with fire. From a peak of bare rocks we saw the wide land of the Iroquois Indians, with the great valley of the long Canada river. Lakes, high hills, and deep valleys, where wild men hunt elk, moose and bears, were around us. It is a terrible wilderness of mountains and game."—*Old Manuscript.*

TRADITION OF CARBUNCLES.

Some of the early explorers of these mountains with great solemnity affirmed that they saw, hanging from the crags, great carbuncles, whose brilliancy was glorious to behold. This report attracted the attention of adventurers; and several exploring parties have visited these mountains, with the hope of finding rich and rare gems of great value; but, though various attempts have been made to gain possession of these wonders, none have yet been obtained. It is recorded that some of these *carbuncle hunters* have taken with them spiritual advisers to "lay" or "exorcise" the supernatural guardians of the mountain wealth; but all to no purpose. In an old White Mountain record is found a journal of a carbuncle seeker:—"Hearing that a glorious carbuncle had been found under a large shelving rock, difficult to obtain, placed there by the Indians who killed one of their number, that an evil spirit might haunt the place, we went up Dry river, with guides, and had with us a good man to lay the evil spirit; but returned sorely bruised, treasureless, and not even saw that *wonderful sight.*" Recently no mention has been made of wonderful carbuncles; and there is a tradition that an old Indian pronounced a curse, called *"the red man's curse,"* upon the pale-faced gem-seekers; and when he died his last wish was (to save his spirit the trouble of keeping the mountain-treasure from the white man's polluting touch, by enchantment), that the Great Spirit would send a black storm of fire and thunder, and splinter the crags, and roll down the carbuncles with mighty avalanches, and bury them deeply in the valleys, beneath the ruins of rocks and trees.

THE INDIAN GHOST.

There are those now living in the shadow of these mountains who seem to believe that, every "fall of the leaf," on a certain night, a supernatural brightness glows upon a particular crag, and the giant ghost of an Indian warrior, fancifully arrayed in a black bear-skin war-robe, with a bloody stone tomahawk, and a broken horn-beam bow, may be seen dancing in the wind, by the light, to the measure of his self-sang dirge. At such times the snow disappears from off the rocks around; but no mountaineer has ever been found capable of climbing the ice-crags, to satisfy the curiosity whether or not fire-marks may at times be found.

LOST SPIRITS' LOOKING-GLASSES.

If a humble addition may here be allowed, might not these wonderful carbuncles have been merely rocks seen at a distance, covered with water or ice, with the sunlight reflected to favor the delusion? Or, if we need a tincture of the miraculous, perchance some of Darby Field's Muscovy glass was so arranged by the mountain genii, as to answer for looking-glasses, in which lost Indian spirits might see themselves. But even this isinglass, of such size, cannot be found, for a wonder. Has not the brother of the speculative Yankee who attempted to whittle the north pole up for tooth-picks, spirited this even away, that it might be devoted to mechanical purposes by the utilitarian age? Speak, ye who can say!

ROGERS AND HIS RANGERS.

The night of October 3d, 1765, the St. Francis Indians, at their village on the bank of the river for which their tribe was named, held a grand war-dance. Fair maidens and brave young warriors where there, with light hearts; and wildly in the night rose their triumph-song, as they swung in air the scalp-locks of a hundred pale-faces. They dreamed not that a spy was in their ring, and that ere another sun the three pale-faced captives, who sorrowfully listened to their barbaric jubilee, would wade through their warm blood, and be far on the long trail over the mountains. Robert Rogers, dispatched, with two hundred (some historians say five hundred) tried rangers, through the long wilderness, to chastise these Indians for that in celebration of which they this night held the great dance, was there; and when daylight returned, their village was in ashes, and hundreds slept the sleep of death. Belknap, in his New Hampshire History, says: "The houses of these Indians were well furnished, and their church was richly adorned with plate." Two hundred guineas, with a silver image weighing eight pounds, and a great quantity of rich wampum, were taken from this church as lawful plunder. Satisfied with his work, Rogers made his retreat up the St. Francis river, intending with his men to pass the carrying-place to Magog Lake, thence home to the south part of Laconia: (N.H.). The snow came on deep, and, being pursued by the remnant left after the destruction of that Indian village, several of their number were killed; and, after wandering many days,

they became scattered, and many perished by hunger
and cold. The early settlers of Cohos (Coos) found
relics of this ill-fated party, and later, among the White
Mountains sad vestiges arise in the twilight of tradition; and, faithful to the living history of this famous
mountain, they shall have record.

SILVER IMAGE, WAMPUM, AND MONEY

In the retreat and pursuit following the result of
Rogers' expedition most of the rangers followed their
leader's command, while small detached parties, throwing off all martial restraint, made independent homeward trails for themselves. One small party of nine,
leaving the waters running northward, passed the high-
lands, and came upon a stream that evidently fell into
the Connecticut. Here they resolved to strike that river
at the head of the falls (now called Fifteen Miles Falls),
southerly of Upper Cohos, and, following up the stream
(John's river) that came from the "Crystal Hills," pass
over to the valley of the Amonoosuc, and through the
Notch, homeward. This party had expected to meet a
detachment on the Connecticut, from old No. 4 (now
Charleston N.H.), with supplies; and, being disap-
pointed in this, in a most travel-worn and destitute condition, after waiting several days they yielded to the
guidance of an Indian runner, who offered to conduct
them to the great pass of the "Crystal Hills." They did
not dream that this Indian was acting false, by know-

ing the prophecy of the gray-headed old Indian, who
in the St. Francis church said to the plunderers of the treasure there, *"The Great Spirit will scatter darkness upon
the path of the pale-faces!"* How literally this prophecy
was fulfilled, the end shows more clearly than facts seen
in the mist of dreams. This Indian guide led his charge
up the Connecticut to the mouth of the next river, which
he called Singrawack,* and from thence they followed
up to near the foot of the White Mountains, where he
left them. This little party had in charge the plunder
taken from the Indian church, and to him who bore the
treasure, the Indian gave a rude birch-bark map, de-
scriptive of their route thence. The reason given by
the Indian guide for going no further was pretended
fear that the Great Spirit would kill him; if he left his
footprints in the shadow of the great snowy Agiochook.
The ranger who received the birch map did not notice
an apparently accidental scratch given him on the back
of his hand by the guide on the receipt of the map; but
when his hand began to swell, suspicion rested upon
the false guide. Symptoms of poison became strik-
ingly apparent, and the increasing inflammation gave
speed to his blood, and fear mingled with pain pressed
madness into his brain, and with frightful shrieks of

---

* This name signifies *"Foamy Stream of* The White Rock." In
memory of a great hunter, *Israel Stark*, who long ago hunted in the
valley of this stream, it has been called Israel's river. This river

rage he rushed to a high rock, and, throwing himself down, was dashed to pieces. The gloom of death in their midst, combined with the startling circumstances, was like a black night-shadow upon the future prospects of this little party; and, holding a brief council, the decision was that their companion came to his death by a slight wound of a rattlesnake's fang, designed by their Indian guide. With the remembrance of the Indian prophecy fresh in mind, they resolved to bury the mangled remains of their mate, with his knapsack containing the stolen treasure, carefully in a rude cave, where the red hunter dared not leave his footmarks.

According to old tradition, of that party of nine but one ever reached the settlement below the mountains. Being misled by their false guide, they miscalculated as to the certainty of passing down the mountain notch; and, being the distance of two river valleys to the northward of the point from which they might have passed through safely, they wandered many days in vain attempt to attain their object, and, after extreme suffering from hunger, and the rigorous storms of approaching winter, one only arrived to tell the sad story of misery and death. This ragged and forlorn-looking mortal had with him six knives, and in his bloody knapsack was a

turns the machinery of the thriving village of Lancaster, as it passes through, on its foaming track to the broad Connecticut, with which it mingles a mile below Lancaster village

piece of human flesh, of which for the last eight days
he declared he had eaten to support the flickering spark
of life that now but faintly burned within him.

RANGERS' RELICS FOUND.

When the early hunters came to the valley of the
Cohos (meadow of pines), on a pine-tree standing up
in a wild gorge, on what the Indians call Singrawack,
was a barkless spot, whereon was a curious mingling
of storm-worn hieroglyphical characters. Near this was
found the remains of a military dress—rusty buttons
&c., with a gun-barrel lock, rotten stock, and a small
copper kettle. In another place, while digging away
the rubbish at the foot of a steep bank near which a
block-house had lately been erected, in place of an expected spring of water were found six old gun-barrels,
and what appeared to be a pile of knapsack, containing
a quantity of frogs and fish-bones. A certain old hunter,
by the delusive influence of three similar dreams, fancied that he should become wealthy by untiring search
for precious treasures among the White Hills. One day,
while engaged in his exploring operations, a terrible
mountain storm obliged him to seek shelter under an
overhanging cliff. While there he noticed, back in a
dark corner, among the shadows of this rude cave, several flat stones piled up in a manner too curious to be
natural. On examination under this pile, he found a
rusty old hatchet, and a roll of birch-bark, neatly en-

cased in wild-bees' wax. A disagreeable stench rose
from the damp mould within the crevice wherein these
relics were secured, and a silent fear of he knew not
what caused the old hunter to instinctively withdraw
from further examination. Within the birch-bark roll
he found a parchment, formed of an Indian-tanned
fawn-skin, on which were written many characters,
which to the unlettered hunter were mysterious. He
carried his unaccountable prize to the nearest settlement, and, being void of all antiquarian spirit, sold it
to a distiller of spirits for two quarts of potato-whis-
key. Here the mysterious manuscript disappeared, and
by many it is believed to have been burned with the
whisky-shop in 1804. Be this as it may, the old hunter
now fancied he could lead a party of treasure-seekers
to the hiding-place of the silver image, and other treasure supposed to be there somewhere, in sacred keeping of the mountain genii. Ere we proceed to notice
the party in search for the secret of the mountain cave,
we will note other wild traditions, that stalk before us
like gigantic shadows, speaking from the past, saying,
*"Whether false or true, time-honored fictions, in this
imaginative age, are as much of a legal tender for the
literary world, as dry modern facts."*

STRANGE SIGHTS SEEN.

Years previous to a settlement near these mountains,
a hunter brought from thence what was considered by

many a vague report of a strange vision seen. He was alone, and what part imagination had to do with what he fancied to be true, judge ye who please. He was camping far up among the White Hills, on a stream called by the natives "Singrawack," one night, when his camp-fire burned low, and a dreamy restlessness mocked his desire to enjoy profound sleep; and to his sight, on a background of deep blue sky, arose the craggy mountain, enlivened by the magic splendor of a moonlit night. The mountain's northern side was hid in its own dark shadow; but silvery moonbeams were glittering upon its pointed rock, and around its top hung a still, thick mist. Above the murmuring of mountain waterfalls rose a strange noise indistinctly; but, being of a stout heart, he heeded it not, save as the ominous hoot of some solitary owl, or the lone howl of a hungry wolf, giving zest to his hopeless employment by keeping up his spirits with a rude serenade for the moonlit night. The hunter's nerves were like steel, but a fanciful influence changed the mist to a great stone church, and within this was an altar, where from a sparkling censer rose a curling wreath of incense-smoke, and around it lights dispersed a mellow glow, by which in groups before that altar appeared a tribe of savages kneeling in profound silence. A change came in the wind; a song loud and long rose as a voice-offering to the Great Spirit; then glittering church-spire, church and altar, vanished, and down the steep rock trailed a long line of strange-looking men, in solemn silence. Before all, as borne by some airy sprite, sported a glittering image of silver, which in deep shadows changed to fairy shape, and, with sparkling wings, disappeared in the rent rocks. A loud laugh of brutal triumph, combined with the strange vision, startled to consciousness the hunter; and, musing on what had passed, he rekindled his fire by the light of morning over the eastern mountains.

Another report declares that, not far from the period of which we speak, another hunter was startled from profound sleep in the dead of night by most hideous screechings, as of a man in the last agonies of extreme torture. At intervals, through the remainder of the night, above the roar of the mountain stream rose strange noises, either through fancy or reality.

Connected with the same odd train, so much in keeping with the spirit of wild legendary adventure, comes another account, that, in a superstitious, witchcraft age, might cause some credulous ones to become confident. There once came a great storm, out of which came a voice, saying; *"That pagan treasure from St. Francis may not remain a secret to adventure till the Great Spirit's thunder dies on the crags of Agiochook."* When these words were pronounced, the apparition of a skeleton Indian, with ribs like loud-sounding harp-strings, was followed by an armed train of pale-faces; an Indian village was burning, and from the blood and ruins of the fire-lit night a soldier appeared, bearing a silver image, money and wampum, away to the woods. After thus much of the wonderful, the precise locality of the treasure, with a power to do away the influence of enchantment, was reserved for the genius of

THE OLD FORTUNE-TELLER.

The history of *"image memory,"* as connected with these bald peaks, has connected with it the old Fortune-teller, who, by her wonderful disclosures, had the credit of being leagued with the spirits of another world. By her high pretensions, she held the power of divination, and among her superstitious votaries passed for what no mortal is. She had a magic stone, said to have been found in a cave among the mountains, and possessing marvellous supposed virtues. This was considered as a priceless treasure by Indian Magi—fit offering to the Great Spirit. Such was the *"favoring star"* that ruled her strange destiny, that from this stone she pretended to read events of the past and future. Her home was a rude mud hovel, in a by-place, where she was visited by but few, save those who ignorantly believed in her magical power. She sought no mortal sympathy, and busied her loneliness in seeking poison-herbs, which were potent helps to her power. Many believed she could blast the hopes of youth by one withering look of displeasure, change the boldest heart to one of fear, and dry, by one wave of her hand, the blood of ambition in the veins of manhood; and, in short, her victims believed her immortal. Her art was solicited as an aid to the accomplishment of the object had in view by the fortune adventurers.

SEARCH FOR THE IMAGE, MONEY, AND WAMPUM.

The hunter who had found the hatchet and bark roll, with four other adventurers, made ready for a search for the silver image, &c., with the old fortune-teller as a figure-head for the enterprise. She agreed, if the party would but abide her arrangements, they should be successful. Accordingly, her labelled phials, apparatus for burning drugs, smattering of mystic words in an unknown tongue, with the *magic stone,* completed for her a fancied latent power, equal in confidence to try skill with the mighty magician of all foul incantations. She pretended the treasure they sought was under the influence of strong enchantment; and, by a fancied combination of astrology, alchemy and divination, she declared that the next night the situation of the stars would be favorable for their purpose. With pick, bar, spade and axe, together with the old Fortune-teller's spiritual weapons, early in the morning this little party started for the mountains, with sufficient imaginary power to lay the ill-will of the most fearful hobgoblins that ever walked in darkness. Once in motion, with their physical and spiritual apparatus in view, a moderate sketch of fancy might startle the supposition that, with individual assurance, their object was to dare the infernal regions, and poison the imps with a refined portion of the old fortune-teller's phialled-up venom. The old hunter who had found the relics had but little faith in her art; yet his love of adventure had led him to brave the ridicule of those who were but slightly tinctured in mind by superstition, while he at the same time cherished an injury against her that was deeply hacked in his memory. He was an old bachelor, and he believed the old fortune-teller had been guilty of poisoning the one of his choice, to gratify the ill-will cherished by an unwelcome rival; and he had been heard to say, *"Give me but time to prove that the old hag is not invincible by her covenant with the devil, and I die contented."* In sullen silence he marked out their path; and, as he trailed along with his rifle laid across one arm, with a hunting-knife, suspended by a leathern girdle, in its shaggy bear-skin sheath, it would have been pleasant to those who are gratified by studying variety of character to have noted his proud bearing. He had already had hard words with the old fortune-teller, and now there was meaning in the stern expression of his weathered-tanned face. Time had deeply furrowed his brow, and habit had thereon contracted an eternal scowl, which, with a cold, fixed stare, as he plodded onward, told of a design that was steeling his heart for its accomplishment.

It is sufficient to hasten forward to the concluding scene, by noting that the old fortune-teller and the hunter had a falling out, as they halted to eat their "cold lunch;" and, drawing his knife, he swore he would know on the spot whether she was in league or not with invisible powers. Bloodshed was doubtless alone prevented by timely interference of others of the party, and she declared she could find that treasure without the hunter's aid, and would not proceed further under his guidance. From this point she became guide; and, having assumed this right, such scrambling over bush and log, through swamp and brook, was seldom undergone before, perchance, by one who on winged thought could compass space by the art of magic. Much of the activity of better days had been kept alive by the old fortune-teller, by her active habits, through woods and fields in search for roots and herbs; and either on the uprising vapor from broken phials, or by the transforming power of magic, they arrived, about sunset, near where accounts had fixed the location of the treasure. The *precise spot* was soon pointed out by the aid of a peculiar rod, and the "*magic stone*;" and all things were prepared for successful search, when that night the position of the "*favoring star*" might make known the exact moment. The night threatened to be dark and showery; and, with gloomy forebodings of an uprising tempest, the wind roared mournfully over the lone wilderness; and high up among the rocks, in a narrow copse of scrub spruce, glimmered a little, wavering fire. Around that fire, within range of the fitful glare it sent out upon the starless night, was the male portion of that treasure-seeking party (excepting the old hunter), gravely watching every motion of the old fortune-teller, as, with a jabberish jargon of discords, she tended a pot of simmering herbs. Lazily the hours crept on towards midnight, and all wondered why the old hunter did not come; and, at last, with all things ready, the female genius gave the watchword "ready!" and next followed the order "strike!" with the caution not to cease searching till she gave warning that the spell was broken, and the treasure within their grasp. Then arose the din of spade and bar, and the clinking pickaxe struck sparks from the flinty rocks, as the diggers toiled on; and, busy as a bewitching spirit in a gale of wind, the old fortune-teller fluttered about, now here, now there, strewing the midnight air with volatile odor from an uncorked phial, urging the men to unremitting diligence, and ever and anon waving her wand through the black night, with a wild muttering of strange words accompanying. Wrought up to the highest pitch by avaricious excitement, nerved by mingled fear and hope, they had little heeded the terrific warfare that the elements were gathering in the distance to break in fury about their heads. The dolorous murmuring of the roused wind, that at dark swept over the groaning woods, had now increased to a heavy gale, that wildly whirled about the naked rocks, above and below and the lightning, that had long been advancing with a wider curve over the front of the on-coming thunder-cloud, now changed the black darkness to a mighty heaving mass of liquid fire; then the roar of the thunder burst among the craggy rocks, echoing in continued peals, shaking the very mountain with a noise like the voice of an upheaving earthquake. A terrible crash followed, like the falling of a hundred towering pines; and, with the flood loosened from the clouds by the shock, rocks and trees rolled in fearful destruction down the mountain gorge. The flickering light of their uncertain pine torch disappeared in the wind, and between the vivid flashes that in quick succession followed appeared a slight glimpse of total chaos. Consternation seized those men; and, hesitating, the voice of the old fortune-teller screamed, amid the dire confusion of thunder, wind and water. *"Dig, men, dig!* the power of light or darkness cannot harm you! This raging is the powerful influence of strong enchantment! Dig!—*dig!*—the treasure must come forth amid the convulsions of the elements!" Ere she had finished speaking, another flash revealed the diggers standing, like pale ghosts, reckless of her com-

mand. Like a wild fury, she leaped into the hollow
among moved rocks, and, with one despairing shriek,
fell to work, cursing her companions. A loud, shrill
whoop rose up with the din of the storm, in mocking
answer to her rage; and when next a blue twinkling
flame spread over the black rocks a ghostly light, a
giant form arose from the mist, hurled over the precipice kettle and phial, and, taking the *"magic stone"* in
both hands, when next a flash lit up the scene, a fierce
grin appeared upon a visage strangely like the old
hunter's face,—a deep groan followed,—again elec-
tric fire lit up rock and cloud; and, with a wild, loud
laugh, the phantom of the mist was seen dragging the
old fortune-teller by her hair towards the brink of the
precipice. Our heroes of "image-seeking memory"
waited to see no more. Fancying the powers of the
earth and air combined against their enterprise, they
made random leaps, through the darkness, down precipitous rocks, and anon lighted for a moment by a flash
on the steep and dangerous way, arrived in the low valley, wet, weary, bruised, and frightened. Next morning the sun rose clear over the mountains, lighting the
mist that hung on the glittering rocks; and where the
last night's battle had been, upon bush, rock and moss,
sparkled a thousand raindrops, like priceless gems in
nature's glorious crown. The fate of the old fortune-
teller and hunter to this day remains a mystery; but the

track made by the scathing lightning that fearful night may now be seen; and the traditions preserved by the simple-minded settlers near associate with their importance a saintly fear, when they call to mind the circumstances of that night. Around that time-honored spot, strange wailings may now be heard when the wind is high; and some fancy that a giant Indian spirit watches near, and, with goodly semblance of sincerity, the same believe that, bound in some dark cavern, the old fortune-teller and hunter in spirit dwell together in torment.

THE OLD BRASS PLATE.

About the year 1802, a curious plate, covered with hieroglyphical inscriptions, of apparently ancient date, was found under a rock near the top of Mount Washington. When it was placed there, or by whom, is yet a profound mystery. There was through the plate a hole, and a piece of rusty copper, that appeared to be a bolt once used to secure it to the rock. According to tradition, this brass was of irregular shape, having been apparently much eaten by rust; and, from its real appearance, the characters were said to be in an unknown tongue; and, in short, of very imperfect and doubtful import. This was found by an explorer, or hunter; and, being carried to the then new settlement of Jackson, below the mountain, for a while created a short-lived excitement, and at last disappeared entirely.

DISCOVERY OF NOTCH.

By record it appears that this remarkable defile was known to the aborigines, but was never used by them as a crossing-place for their captives, or as a war-path, till white explorers in part wiped from their moral vision the dark superstition that such approach to Agiochook would be deemed by the Great Spirit pardonless sacrilege. For many years after it was known to the first hunters this Notch became forgotten or neglected, till the year 1771, when it was re-discovered by two hunters, *Nash* and *Sawyer.* They drove a moose up a wild mountain stream, surrounded by towering crags; and, with the belief that it was a deep gorge, surrounded behind by mountains, they followed, animated by the thought of making an easy conquest of their intended victim. Imagine their disappointment when they found their purpose thwarted by tracing the foot-prints of the moose along an ancient Indian trail, over high precipices, to a little meadow quite on the other side of the mountain! These hunters published this interesting discovery, and were rewarded by the tract of land, northerly from the Notch, known as "Nash and Sawyer's Location."

DESCRIPTION OF NOTCH, ETC.

The Notch is a narrow rent, extending more than two miles between towering crags. This is doubtless the mighty work of some overwhelming internal convulsion; or, perchance, the deluge here tore mountains asunder. The entrance of this wonderful chasm is about twenty-two feet wide, forming in itself a strange natural gateway, with high mountain fragments piled up on either side, receding as you go down, till their tops reach the clouds. From a little beaver meadow the Saco river rises northerly from this gateway, and, struggling down its narrow bounds, shares with the road its wild gulf; and, having passed through the mountain, bears its tribute onward to the ocean. Words cannot describe faithfully the magnificent scenery of the Notch. This wonderful display of Almighty power creates invariably sensations of awe and mortal weakness. Passing low down between the ruins of mountains rent to their foundation, the tourist will notice a beautiful waterfall on the left, that, foaming over a series of rocks, falls in one place, nearly perpendicular, eight hundred feet. This was by Dr. Dwight very appropriately named *Silver Cascade,* and is said to be one of the finest waterfalls in the world. Below, a short distance, on the same side, falls another stream, clear and beautiful. This, from having worn a channel deeply into the rock, is called *The Flume.* In one place this stream leaps a hundred feet; and its whole course from the clouds down is foamy and wild. For two thirds of the year a more desolate place can hardly be imagined than this Notch. Dismal winds moan through the leafless trees, and through the fissures of the rocks; and methinks the poor storm-bound traveller here in fancy has heard the genii of the mountain, sending through this gorge a deafening chorus of most frightful music. Woe, then, to poor mortality, when the snow falls fast, and the king of tempests rides on the wings of the hurricane through the clouds, armed with winter's cold, blinding sleet, and avalanches of ice!

The *first settler through the Notch* was Col. Whipple, from Portsmouth, N.H. He came up in the year 1772, and he was at that time enabled to get his cattle up through the Notch by means of teacles and ropes, as the hunter's path was over several precipices, now shunned by the travelled way. All the way through the northern wilderness of Laconia (now N.H.), with the needful means of civilization with him, he came, scaled the crags that hang around that mighty rent through mountains, and by his enterprise earned the honor of being the first white man who made a permanent settlement in the township of Dartmouth (now Jefferson).

The *first female* through the Notch was one who in her old age was known as *"Granny Stalbird."* She came up with Col. Whipple in 1776, as his servant-girl. Afterwards she married, became a widow; since which, learning of the Indians the virtue of roots and herbs, she became a noted doctress, and was famous in all this new country for her skill. After enjoying life for nearly a full century, she died, leaving her name in the memory of many pleasantly cherished; and the history of a vast rock, that long ago tumbled down from the mountains, bears the name "Granny Stalbird's Rock." One time, while passing on her professional duties through the Notch, she was overtaken by a terrible storm; and darkness coming on, with torrents of water from the clouds, that swelled to a fearful height the wild mountain streams, she sought shelter under this rock, and laid there through a sleepless night, with the doleful music of water, wind and wolves, around her. The habits of this useful old doctress were quite masculine. On foot, or astride of an old horse, she might commonly be seen in the road, hastening from house to house on her errands of mercy. Bad travelling and severe storms, were never insurmountable barriers in her path of usefulness. To do good to the sick was her life; and her God sustained her for long years as a worthy ministering spirit to the afflicted. She needs no monument to her memory more lasting than that which lives in her deeds.

STORY OF NANCY'S ROCK AND BROOK.

On a branch of the Saco, below where the Willey House now stands, a girl perished in 1778. Her sad story is worthy of notice here. Nancy came up through the Notch with Colonel Whipple, soon after his settlement, and a hired servant of his gained her affections.

She learned to place in his fair promises all the confidence of her guiltless heart, and, long cherished as a true friend, the wretch, having moulded her affections completely to his purpose, agreed to go to Portsmouth and be married. They first went to Lancaster, to make necessary preparations for their intended journey through the wilderness. She trusted her lover with the money the colonel had paid her for two years' service, and, false to the common feelings of humanity, he left her, and hastened away on his long journey. There was then no road, and a dense wilderness, thirty miles to the first settlement below the Notch, with only a hunter's path, marked by spotted trees, was to be passed; but Nancy, when aware of her lover's treachery, resolved to follow, at the hazard of life. There was a light snow upon the ground and trees, so that, when she got back to the Colonel's, she was thoroughly drenched, and the cold winds of autumn had chilled her. In vain her friends there tried to dissuade her from following; but persuaded by her determination that her false one would camp at the Notch that night, she thought by travelling without rest she might overtake him there. All night she wandered, and when morning came she reached the spot where the ashes of his camp-fire were yet warm; but he was gone, and in vain, with benumbed hands, she tried to rekindle the fire. Wet, cold and hungry, and excessively wearied by over-exertion, she still clung to the false shadow of a hope that lived in her heart, and made one more desperate effort to—she knew not what.

That branch of the Saco, in the lonely mountain gorge, sings a song that never ends; and by it is a rock that stands as a wasteless monument, silently defying time and storms. These bear the respective names "Nancy's Rock and Brook," and here her body was found, with her head resting upon her hand and cane. Fearing for her safety, as she did not return, her friends followed her the next morning, and found her frozen stiff. The lover of this unhappy girl heard of her horrible death, and, smitten by conscience, became insane, and after a few weeks died a raving madman. This is a concise sketch, as told me by some who, knowing the above facts, yet live to bear record that my description is true.

> Her tragic fate, though horrid to relate,
> Shows how true love controls a woman's fate.

The first goods brought up the Notch was a barrel of rum, which was given to Captain Rosebrook, by a merchant of Portland, on condition he would get it up through the Notch. The captain made record, that after crossing the Saco river twenty-two times, with a horse and two poles, and several men, he succeeded in getting as much of the rum up as *was not used in the enterprise.*

First produce carried down through the Notch was a barrel of tobacco, raised in Lancaster, by one Titus O. Brown. Thus, we see, *rum* and *tobacco* ranked here, where, among many good people of olden times, they were considered absolutely necessary, as first. But, thanks be to reformers, may the day not be far distant when an intemperate use of either shall be looked upon by the public, under the influence of moral persuasion, as an evil to be ranked in the same light with the follies of witchcraft!

FIRST HOUSE IN THE NOTCH.

The Willey House is the oldest building erected in the Notch. This was built in the year 1793, by a Mr. Davis, to accommodate that unfortunate storm-bound traveller, who, from curiosity, or on business, might dare the dangers of this wild pass. Then a little grassy meadow stretched along the bank of the Saco; tall rock-maples, and a towering mountain barrier, rose in the background from this little home of the pilgrim. How like a cool shadow of a great rock was this retreat among the frowning crags! But the thundering avalanche came, and, since August 28th, 1826, the spirit of desolation has brooded over the fated spot. How lonely there is the dirge of the high wind, as it sweeps down that solitary chasm; and the wail of the sunset breeze, with the loud requiem of the on-rushing hurricane, is most mournful, for human bones are there palled in an avalanche's ruins!

AVALANCHES OF THE MOUNTAIN.

Betimes around these *"gray old piles of eternity"* rise heavy black clouds from the four points of heaven, that shroud all "tip-top" in the darkness of night, and cast gloomy shadows on the deep, wild gorges below. Then the invisible genius of storms loosens the howling winds from their secret caverns, down comes the outpouring tornado, the mountain shakes beneath the tramp of the on-rushing tempest, and the rough rocks smoke by the violence of the merciless elements. It is fearful, then, to be high among the rocks, with the roaring hurricane's breath, wildly rushing clouds, heavy thunder-peals, and vivid lightning-flash, mingled in one overwhelming discord around. Then mighty piles of rocks, and acres of forest growth, roll down the mountain side, new streams burst out among the rocks, and thus have these famous peaks become deeply marked by the desolating track of the thundering avalanche. Wide over the valleys below scatter the ruins, like the eruption of a volcano; and loud reverberations among the echoing cliffs, move away like distant thunder. These land-slides generally start near the upper region of scrub vegetation, and, deepening and widening as they rush down, carry with them the forest growth, huge rocks, and all the loose earth, even to the bare granite; and thus, in some remarkable storms, thousands of acres are made desolate, with a thundering noise, like that heard when an earthquake lifts for deliverance. Tourists, on all sides of these mountains, must have noticed long scars, like wide roads, reaching down to the lowlands, that curiously contrast, by their yellow or reddish hues, with the dark, evergreen growth through which they sweep. These are the paths of avalanches.

ORIGIN OF INDIAN FIRE-WORSHIP.

Doubtless the profound veneration which has ever for these old towering piles prevailed among the Indians originated, in part, from these terrible visitations that have here at times shook the foundation of this wild region. The gleam of the lightning flying from cliff to cliff, the voice of the thunder speaking from the black cloud, and the dire confusion of the desolating avalanche, all told of the Great Spirit, to whose almighty power they offered sacrifice with reverence. From the tempest-clouds of Agiochook, for the red hunter, had been sent down fire that shivered the tall pine of the cold, shadowy valley of Amonoosuc; and by it he learned to cook his moose-meat, and warm his wearied limbs. From this gift of fire from the clouds grew up with the tribes of the northern wilderness, according to the imaginative traditionary lore of old, the cel-

ebrated fire-dance, fire-worship, and sacrifice of game
to fire.

DESTRUCTION OF THE WILLEY FAMILY.

Some few instances are on record, and others live in
tradition, of destruction of human life, as, also, of wonderful escapes from death, among these mountains, by
the resistless avalanche. The following account, by its
startling details, first attracts our notice. Some time in
June—before the great "slide" in August, 1826—there
came a great storm, and the old veteran, Abel Crawford,
coming down the Notch, noticed the trees slipping
down, standing upright, and, as he was passing Mr.
Willey's, he called and informed him of the wonderful
fact. Immediately, in a less exposed place, Mr. Willey
prepared a shelter to which to flee in case of immedi-
ate danger; and in the night of August 28th, that year,
he was, with his family, awakened by the thundering
crash of the coming avalanche. Attempting to escape,
that family, nine in number, rushed from the house, and
were overtaken and buried alive under a vast pile of
rocks, earth, trees, and water. By a remarkable circumstance, the house remained uninjured, as the slide
divided about four rods back of the house (against a
high flat rock), and came down on either side, with
overwhelming power. The little meadow there, on the
Saco, was entirely destroyed, and to this day wears a

desert aspect. A commodious two-story hotel has been erected near this spot, and thousands each season come to stand upon the rock that saved that famous old *Willey House,* by turning the force of the thundering avalanche aside. There is, near by, a rude mound of small stones, piled up by strangers, who have visited this spot to see where three children yet sleep in death, beneath the ruins of that fearful night.

NAMES OF THAT FAMILY.

Samuel Willey, Jr., aged 38.		Elbridge G.,	age 7.
Polly L. Willey,	" 35.	Sally,	" 5.
Eliza Ann,	" 13.	David Nickerson,	" 21.
Jeremiah L.,	" 11.	David Allen,	" 37.
Martha G.,	" 9.		

Two first, parents; five next, children; two last, hired men. The three first and three last have been found, and the other three are where the avalanche overtook them that fatal hour.

WONDERFUL ESCAPES.

The Moore's Hist. Col. of N.H., vol. III., p. 226, is found the description of a remarkable escape from death, one dark and rainy night, on the side of Mt. Washington. This we will style *The Destruction of Ethan's Cabin.* The description is as follows: "We were on the north-westerly side of Mt. Washington, August

27th, 1826, about two miles from the top. The storm continued to increase; the very summit seemed to shake in the tempest, and an involuntary dread touched our hearts, as the noise of the hurricane grew louder, and sudden gusts swept over us, and dashed down streams of water upon our frail cabin. Our fire was put out, and, fearing lest delay might be death, we hastened down the mountain, and crossed the Amonoosuc as best we could, which stream was now roaring along like a tremendous cataract. The next morning sun shone out, and we beheld where one slide had the appearance of passing directly over where we had the night before camped." Ethan in his journal says: "God only knows what must have been their fortune, had they remained; and truly thankful they seemed to be for their escape. It seemed really a providential thing their being saved. My *cabin,* where they were stopping, was destroyed, and the *old iron chest* and blankets were all swept away and buried, except a few tattered pieces of blankets that caught on bushes down the river. All else was lost."

ORIGIN OF PEABODY RIVER.

A description of another wonderful escape is found in Rev. H. White's History of New England, page 327. "The father of Olive Peabody, who resided in Andover, Mass., in one of his excursions into New Hampshire met with an adventure which has connected his name with the geography of the country, and which, for that reason, as well as its singularity, may, perhaps, with propriety, be mentioned here. He was passing a night in the cabin of an Indian, situated on the height between the Saco and the Androscoggin rivers. The inmates of this rude dwelling were awakened in the course of the night by a loud noise, and had scarcely time to escape, before the hut was swept away by a torrent of water rushing impetuously down the hill. On reconnoitering the spot, they found that this torrent had burst out suddenly from a place where there was no spring before." This is supposed to date back to the origin of the branch of Peabody river, that runs in front of the Glen House, and hence came its name.

DARBY FIELD'S SECOND VISIT.

This extravagant description, by one who occupies a prominent place as an early explorer, is deemed worthy of record as a curiosity. It might as properly have been noticed in connection with his first visit. Had it then been in my possession, there it would have appeared; but my manuscript, up to this page, now being in proof, here let it be recorded as a worthy relic, rescued by accident from the antiquarian collection of the Massachusetts Historical Society. In a worm-eaten old edition of Winthrop's History, vol. II., page 107, is found the following:

"In his second visit in 1642, Darby Field went up the Saco in birch canoes with his party. He found 10 falls on that river to stop boats, and there were thousands of acres of rich meadow to Pegwagget*, an Indian town. He then went up a hill 30 miles in woody land, and 8 miles up shattered rocks, without trees or grass. The top is 3 or 4 miles over, all shattered stone, and on one end is another rock about a mile high, with an acre on top. At the top of the plain rises 4 great rivers, at the first issue having as much water as will drive a mill. Connecticut from 2 heads at the N.W. and S.W., Saco on the S.E., Amascoggin at the N.E., and Kennebec at the N. by E."

DEATH OF THE ENGLISH BARONET.

From all the hardships of adventurous life among these mountains, but one instance of rashness proving fatal has been known of late years. Many fancy that there is much danger attendant upon a visit to this famous place; but the fact that no serious injury has been suffered by the thousands who here climb to the clouds, with the exception of this solitary case, ought to make assurance double, that, with necessary prudence, danger here is trifling. Much credit is due to the faithful management of the experienced guides who are employed, for the benefit of company, at the hotels around the mountains.

* Conway.

In the autumn of 1851, late in October, a young English baronet visited the White Mountain Notch, and, notwithstanding snow was on all the bald peaks above, he determined to visit the top of Mount Washington. He could not be dissuaded from the rash attempt, go he would. A guide went with him to the top of Mount Clinton from Gibbs', and, finding the snow deep, and the wind rough and wintry, the experience of the guide warned his better judgment that it was highly imprudent to go further; and, having said all he could to discourage going forward, he turned back, supposing the Englishman would soon follow. Night came on, but no Englishman, and early the next morning a party followed. They tracked him to the top rock of Mount Washington, to near where the north end of the Tiptop House now stands. Fabyan's house was then standing, and being westerly in full view down the Amonoosuc valley, he started down apparently with the calculation to reach that point. Down where D. Field, in his first visit, said, *"There was such a precipice as we could scarcely discern the bottom,"* they followed his trail. They found where he fell many times, and at last marks of blood were on the snow, and from thence he appeared to drag himself along. In the valley of the Amonoosuc they found his body, mangled, and nearly naked. He was lying on his face in a little stream. In the remains of his clothing were found thirty dollars in gold, and a large check, payable in New York city.

DEATH-LEAP OF THE MOOSE AND DOG.

On an eastern spur of the White Mountains is a beetling crag, down which a hunter once drove a moose,
and his dog, pressing eagerly on the track of his intended victim, followed, and both were mingled in one
mangled mass of bones, flesh, and blood. There is a
tradition of a man who during the early survey of the
township of Sherburne, was hired to climb that ledge
over which the moose and dog leaped, and his reward
was to be the best lot of land in the township. He succeeded in accomplishing the daring feat, and the object of his hire has since, by the nerve that caused him
to not look back or falter in the attempt, become a pleasant home for a second generation of his enterprising
name.

INDIAN EXILE, PEALSUCEP.

A sun's journey up the Androscoggin from its mouth,
in a wild glen, by the shore of a little lake that was
curiously surrounded by a fanciful setting of evergreen
verdure, stood the wigwam of a young hunter. His name
was Pealsucep, and a pretty young squaw was the light
of his rude home. They were happy together, for the
Great Spirit had smiled upon their love, and given them
a son, a bright-eyed little boy, who filled the hearts of
his parents with unclouded hope. When he walked upon
the lake shore, and picked curious stones, and danced
merrily among the wild-flowers, it showed the fulness

of his youthful joy to their hearts, and they were happy. One day, when the hunter was away to the chase on the hills, a pale-faced stranger came to his cabin, treated his squaw rudely, and in pretended sport gave his boy a toss out into the lake to see him swim ashore. The little fellow struggled manfully, and regained the shore amid the shouts of the pale-faced sailor, who then offered the squaw drink from a bottle, and departed. Pealsucep returned, and the little lad soon after grew sick, and, lingered three days, died. The squaw told the story of the pale-face, to which the hunter listened silently, with downcast look. He went often to the grave of his little boy, and made fit offering there, that his journey might be swift and bright beyond the sunset. But from this time there was a black cloud upon the path of Pealsucep; the cruel fire of jealousy was kindled with undying rage in the deep feelings of his spirit, and in vain did his guiltless squaw declare her innocence. Like a tender flower that nestles for protection against wind and storm in the shade of some defiant mountain pine, she felt her support was gone; a blight came over her hopes, and she died. Silently and tearfully Pealsucep laid her by the side of her little boy. Two moons passed away; his tribe became indignant, called to council, and the gray-headed old chief sent for Pealsucep, and said: *"You have sent your squaw away before the Great Spirit called her. You are a swift hunter and brave; but never make a foot-mark among the hunters of your tribe after to-morrow's sun, unless you take the cripple that lives by the river for your squaw."* Pealsucep looked upon the cripple, shook his head, and ere sunset had gathered a pile of pine-knots near his cabin door. When darkness that night came down upon the lone wilderness, he kindled his knot-pile, and by its light laid upon it the bodies of his squaw and son, and, leaving them there to consume, bounded away to the gloom of the thick woods, filling the night with fearful shrieks of anguish. With the morning light he returned. His hunting-dress was in tatters, his hair strangely tangled, and, silently gathering the ashes of those he once loved into a rude bark-box, up towards the mountain he turned his lone steps, and made for himself a new path in the wilderness. Tradition says that upon a foaming stream, in the shadow of the "Great Spirit's" home, the ashes of that squaw and her boy now repose, with a rude stone pile to mark the spot. What of Pealsucep? He made a vow; and, if tradition be true, the Great Spirit heard it. He dared His displeasure; and, high up among the clouds, breathed a promise to the *Invisible Influence* of storms; and most faithfully a whisper came to his spirit. Deathless hate and untiring revenge against his tribe and the pale-faces were the burden of his wishes. For years he appeared to be the incarnate embodiment of a destroying genius, that walked in the wind, and silently speeded the arrow of death on its fatal mission, till his tribe dwindled away, and the pale-faces abandoned their settlement at the mouth of the Kennebec. By tradition he was instrumental in destroying the war-party at Lewiston Falls, by a false light, set, as they supposed, by their runners who went forward to prepare camping-ground. This light, instead of being set at the head of the falls, was set down below; and, coming down the river after dark, taking the light as guide for turning their canoes ashore, all went down, and perished. At a certain block-house he shot several sentinels, and at last was himself wounded, by the stratagem of a sentry at that post. He this time crawled away to the river bank, floated across, and, filling his wound with moss, lived for a long time on beech-leaves and roots, and recovered. He took several prisoners, for which he received of the Jesuits a bounty; and among others there was a little girl by the name of Mary Crager, whose fate adds a curious page to this list of mountain relics. This Indian, according to tradition, once found, while climbing a spur of these mountains, a quantity of *fine silver ore*. He was scrambling up a steep ledge, where, to facilitate his ascent, he took hold of a bush that came up by the roots, revealing to his wondering gaze hanging pieces of ore that appeared to have oozed out in its richness from the crevices of the cliff. This Indian in 1779 was very old and feeble; his great age made him quite harm-less, and he lived in a shadow of the Great Spirit's home; and there his bones now moulder, by a rushing mountain stream, that signs an endless song for *three*— the little Indian boy, his mother, and old Pealsucep, the exile.

WHITE-MOUNTAIN HERMIT.

Thomas Crager was the first white man who ever dwelt near the White Mountains. He lived at a time so unfortunate that law supposed if a person could not swim, when arrested, they could send their spirit into the body of some neighbor's cat, and walk the night doing mischief. Accordingly his wife was executed as a witch; and this sad event bowed his spirit low in the shadow of grief. But one little ray of hope beamed through the night of his soul; this was his love for his motherless little girl. One evening, when a number of little children were at play near a wood, suddenly the cry arose that an Indian had carried off little *Mary Crager.* Nerved by the spirit of desperation, the last tie binding this unfortunate man to civilized life was now severed; and, equipped for the chase, he shaped his course for the unpathed wilderness. Near the White Mountains he came to an Indian village, but, failing to find the object of his search there, he took advantage of the native superstition existing among the red hunt-ers of that wild region, and went up to dwell among the rocks, where, undisturbed, he for a longtime lived, to savage fancy, as an adopted son of the Great Spirit. Unannoyed by savage neighbors, fish were plenty, abundance of game lived on every wooded steep and shady glen, and in his habitation of solitude he was lord of the realm he trod. The crystal waters and pure air of the mountains gave him health and strength; and as years rolled away, void of the exciting passions of busy life, he grew old slowly, for a glimmering hope yet bound him to earth. In his intercourse with his red neighbors, he was respected on account of his home being, like an eagle's, perched among the rolling clouds; and, having learned that a little pale flower had long been in the possession of a gray-headed old Indian, who made his dwelling-place alone, distant from his tribe, he sought for him, and found what strengthened his fears. He found, in the possession of this Indian, a piece of what he knew to be the dress of his little girl, the evening she was stolen away. The Indian was now very old and feeble, and, raising his trembling hand when Crager came into his presence, the flash of vengeance rekindled his dim eyes, and it was a long time ere he could so calm his fears as to gain from him in broken English the sought-for information. In the end he learned from the Indian, by promising to instruct him in the use of a gun, that the child he sought was sold to the Jesuits, on a big river towards the sunrise, and that now she was a tall woman, if living. It is sufficient for the purpose of these pages* that, after a series of curious adventures, Crager succeeded in finding his daughter, among the eastern Indians of the Abnakis tribe, married, and living like a native squaw. He found also in the possession of old Pealsucep specimens of silver, and learned from him the tradition referred to in our notice of the exile; and, by making a solemn promise to bury his remains, when dead, by the side of his squaw and boy, he received a rude description of the locality of that mine. But to this day the world, perchance, is no richer, save in fancy, for the tin, and lead, and *silver*, with which these mountains abound. Perchance more silver may some day be made by working in tin veins of Jackson, and the lead mines of Shelborne, than can be realized by magic applications for hidden treasures and silver mines.

WHITE-MOUNTAIN HOTELS.

The world-wide reputation of these mountains, gained since they were first called *"Chrystal Hills,"* in 1631, yearly calls to their airy heights and shaded sylvan retreats thousands from all parts of the world, that in this mountain land they may for a season shake off the perplexities of business life, and freely receive the

* In a forthcoming edition of The Indian Traditions and Legends of Agiochook, this tradition and its details will appear, perchance.—AUTHOR

invigorating influence of health and comfort. For the accommodation of these numerous visitors, mammoth hotels have been erected in the most attractive localities; and, being managed on the most approved city style, the *"Alpine House,"* at Gorham Station, "Thomson's *Glen House,"* "Gibbs' *Notch House,"* and *"The White-Mountain House,"* give satisfactory evidence of their deserved popularity by the literal patronage seasonably bestowed upon each. Within a pleasant drive of the base of these mountains are delightful villages (Conway, on the Saco; Gorham, on the Androscoggin; Lancaster, on the Connecticut, and Whitefield, near the Amonoosuc), where the free circulation of fresh mountain air, and pure water, foaming cold from icy indentations among snowy cliffs, afford to all who come and tarry a pleasant and healthful contrast to the sickly, pent-up city street, where floats a hot atmosphere of pestilence and death.

DWELLING-PLACE IN THE CLOUDS.

The possibility of erecting a permanent summer home for a man on the top crag of Mount Washington, was for a long time looked upon with serious doubt, and considered only a fit subject of speculation for the visionary.

The *rude stone cabin,* in our reference to *"The White-Mountain Giant,"* being the first shelter wherein mortals could on this bleak pile of rocks find an artificial resting-place, was ever by the winter storms rendered a most desolate object, though sheltered behind a bold crag. The shingle roof, split down in the woods on the mountain side and packed up on the backs of men, was scattered to the four winds. The levers of the frost, and the wild hurricane, tumbled down the thick stone walls; and every spring a roofless heap of ruins, with a rusty old stove, and the iron chest, was left to tell a sad story of the invisible power that over these towering summits stretches the arm of destruction.

NARZO'S TEMPLE VISION.

A peculiar genius, in 1850, obtained a supposed free-soil title to the top of Mount Washington, with all the privileges and appurtenances to the same belonging; and, erecting gateways upon all the bridle-paths leading up to *"the peaks in the clouds,"* exacted one dollar as toll-fee from each and every person who ascended. He also published a flaming proclamation in the papers of the day, of which this is a true copy:

PROCLAMATION.
FOURTH OF JULY ON
THE WHITE MOUNTAINS

There will be a solemn congregation upon TRIN-ITY HEIGHT, or Summit of Mount Washington, on the Fourth Day of July, A.D. 1851, and 1st year of the

Theocracy, of Jewish Christianity, to dedicate to the coming of the Ancient of Days, in the glory of His Kingdom, and to the marriage of the Lamb; and the literal organization in this generation of the Christian or purple and royal Democracy (let no man profane that name!), or the thousand thousands, and ten thousand times ten thousand of the people of the Saints of the most high God of every nation and Denomination into the greatness of God's kingdom and dominion under the whole heavens; and there will be a contribution for this purpose from all who are willing, in the beauty of holiness, from the dawn of that day.

JOHN COFFIN NAZRO,
Israel of Jerusalem.

The appointed fourth of July was as dark and rainy as any, perhaps, that ever shrouded Mount Washington in wildly-flying clouds; and Nazro, meeting with strong opposition in toll-gathering, relinquished his temple-building designs, and, throwing away his gate-keys to the entrance of this mighty altar, retired to United States service, where, perchance, he may be now plotting the way to fortune among the clouds.

SUMMIT HOUSE ON MOUNT WASHINGTON

The matter-of-fact enterprise of two thorough-going Yankees, J.S. Hall and L. M. Rosebrook, came to the task in 1852, and the above-named house was erected within a few feet of the highest rock of Mount Washington. (See right-hand house in cut on first page.) This structure is of heavy stones, blasted with powder from the mighty paramid on which it stands; and it is twenty-four feet by sixty-four feet, firmly secured to its everlasting foundation by cement, heavy iron bolts; and over the roof are tightened four strong cables. In opposition to the prophecies of the unbelieving, this house stood the storms of winter; and the next summer another house was stone-built, and called the

TIP-TOP HOUSE.

This house was erected by Samuel F. Spaulding & Co., and cement and iron rods hold this monument of daring enterprise, in proud defiance of wind and storm, to the most bleak top crag of Mount Washington. This house is twenty-eight feet wide by eighty-four feet long; and has a deck-roof, whereon the visitor may stand and look down six thousand two hundred and eighty-five feet, on to the vast map spread on every side at his feet. (On the first page of this book this house is seen in the engraving, with a telescope, and three visitors on its roof, under a flag of our country.)

These two houses are unitedly managed by a company of hardy mountaineers, who spare no pains to make this famous resort a true home to the admiring stranger, and a pleasant resting-place to the travel-worn pilgrim. All who seek health and pleasure in this pure mountain climate, or a gratification of curiosity for the wonderful in sublime scenery, will find here ample accommodations for their comfort, both day and night. The changing scenes and reflections connected with every sunset and sunrise, enjoyed from this elevation, are remarkable beyond description. Here too sunlight plays upon the bald rocks, while black storms, armed with wind and thunder, move like the shadows of destroying giants in the habitated regions below. Here the moon, with its starry host, sends down its solemn light upon the gray crags, kindling into a fiery glow a hundred lakes, ponds, rivers, and dashing mountain streams, and strangely enlivening every shady glen with flitting lights and shades for the sombre world. Never did Seer from the land of the pyramids, or Chaldean stargazer, study the heavens from an observatory like this. Ye who would enjoy the sports of stream and forest, come to these mountains! Ye who delight to behold the works of nature in their most sublime flights, come to these mountains! Ye who have a love for novelty and a desire for true pleasure, come and behold God's wisdom displayed in the bold outlines of this gigantic monument of his almighty power! Here the underlying features of grandeur were moulded in imperishable materials by his hand!

MOUNT WASHINGTON CARRIAGE-ROAD.

A company, known as the Mount Washington Carriage-Road Company, was chartered in June, 1853, by the Legislature of New Hampshire, with a capital-stock of fifty thousand dollars. The first day of September, 1853, this company was organized at the *Alpine House,* Gorham, and the following board of directors was chosen: D.O. Macomber, of New York; John M. Woods, R.J. Robinson, and Abner Lowell, of Portland; J.R. Hitchcock and James Dingly, of Gorham; and Baker Burbank, of Shelborne. D.O. Macomber was chosen president; J. R. Lufkin, secretary. This road is to be sixteen feet wide, macadamized, and have a protection-wall, three feet high in dangerous places. A route has been thoroughly surveyed and located, with no greater rise than that of one foot to eight, to the top of Mount Washington, from Thompson's Glen House. The distance by this road varies but little from eight miles, and it is now—June, 1855—in rapid progress towards completion, under the contract of Messrs. Rich & Myers. When a carriage can run to the top of Mount Washington, who can prophesy what a bright new era will dawn upon White-Mountain life? The plan of this road reflects great credit upon the enterprise of the president, D.O. Macomber. The part now located is so calculated as to bring in plain prospect the most varied and wild scenery of the eastern side; and a survey is this season anticipated, by which the road will be located somewhere down the western side; thus completing a carriage-route that for novelty, and unparalleled wonder-exciting location, will not in the western world have an equal.

WHITE MOUNTAINS. OBJECTS OF INTEREST.

On the Eastern side, as the traveler approaches this Alpine region, he will naturally inquire for the objects of interest, to which he wishes to direct his attention. After booking his name for a ride to the summit in the morning, from the Glen House he will pass down southerly along the public road, that connects the eastern and western travel around these mountains. Romantic scenery in its most primitive form everywhere greets attention. A dark old forest rock crumbled from frowning crags—unpathed recesses alone haunted by wild beasts, and deep, wild gorges filled with the thunder rush of wasteless mountain streams, pass like dream changes before the admirer's vision, and about three miles from the Glen brings us to

THE CRYSTAL CASCADE

This is situated on the right hand, in a dark ravine about a hundred rods from the road, and the whole height of the falls is nearly a hundred feet. This fall is broken in its course by projecting rocks, which scatter the water-drops in showers of spray, like liquid silver, upon the surrounding foliage. Over other indentation's of the cliff the water courses down green beds of moss, among stunted trees that struggle for existence in the scanty soil of the fissures and seams of splintered crags. This stream is a tributary sent down from the wild gorges on the southerly side of Mount Washington. Should the adventurous tourist choose this route to the summit, he may find the way rugged and wild, but the change of scenery along the highly romantic gorge will well repay the extra tax upon time and nerve. In one place the

HERMIT'S LAKE,

set like a rich gem in its fanciful frame-work of change-less evergreen, appears, and stopping to enjoy the prospect, the idea of overwhelming wonder rushes upon our spirit in this solitary spot. Across this little lake, high up among the rolling clouds, frowns Mt. Washington, a view of which from this point strangely contrasts with the sparkling rush of noisy water, and the evergreen freshness of surrounding woods. To the westward rises the craggy top of Mt. Washington, and upon all sides, except the outlet through this little lake, known as *The Crystal Stream*, appear high towering cliffs, rendered a picture of desolation by the deep, wide track of many an avalanche. Little spots of verdure, blasted shrubbery, and piles of granite fragment appear below, with the long snow-bank and famous snow-arch*, through which runs the stream that tumbles from the ragged cliff above. Over all mark the mighty pile of mountains that hangs high in bold relief against the sky, and behold the famous

"FALLS OF A THOUSAND STREAMS,"
divided in its descent into silvery streams that in number will warrant the above appellation, and you have a picture of the Mountain Coliseum here faintly referred to, and this also is known as *Tuckerman's Ravine.*

Glen Elise Falls are situated a mile below Crystal Cascade, and considered an object of quite as much interest as that of its rival. It is on the left side of the road, a few rods off, in a deep, dark ravine on Elise River. The water falls in an unbroken sheet about eighty feet. On top of the crag from which this stream is projected, stands a finely rooted old hemlock, that in defiance to the warring elements stretches its shaggy top out a hundred feet above the top of the fall. Up this tree a boy once climbed to the very top, in presence of a party of visitors, and looking down into its fearful vortex of boiling water, nearly two hundred feet, seemed perfectly indifferent concerning his dangerous position. Descending, he was rewarded for this dare-devil feat by an admiring stranger with a York shilling. *"The Lake of the Clouds"* and *"Star Lake,"* set like glitter-

* See description of snow-arch, 14th page

ing diamonds in rough granite frames, on the indentation between the tops of Mt. Washington and Mt. Monroe, will well repay the excursionist for a visit to their romantic shores, distant from tip-top a mile and a half. *"The Gulf of Mexico"* and *"Spaulding's Lake,"* are at least worth a trip from the Atlantic, from all who would look with proud satisfaction upon nature in her sublimest mood. These curiosities are situated near the head of the most northerly branch of Peabody River, between Mt. Washington and Mt. Clay, and are similar in feature to the general outlines of Tuckerman's Ravine. In place, however, of seeing another Fall of a Thousand Streams, the tourist must be content with loosing from the over-hanging cliff vast boulders, that smoking and thundering down deep in the gorge below, are splintered and lost amid the ruins of trees shattered on their downward trail. This little lake, known in its wild bed as *"Spaulding's Lake,"* to appearance was formed by a slide, from the southerly crags of Mt. Adams, has left its rusty, iron track, and piled its ruins in wild confusion high up within the waters of this solitary sheet, may be seen engraved, "J.H.S., 1853."

Many places of interest are yet around this gigantic pile of peaks, but partially explored. The field is open to the spirit of discovery, and besides the piles of cows' bones found last season in the "burnt district," by Mr. Hall, places worthy of note and more relics interesting to the antiquarian will doubtless yearly be brought to light, till these cliffs and gorges, from being an *"unknown certainty,"* become, like a book, thoroughly understood and admired.

On the westerly side of these mountains, the chief objects of interest are the Notch, (already referred to on 48th page,) the Upper and Lower Falls of the Amonoosuc, Mt. Willard, and the carriage ride to its summit. The wilderness valley stretches over thousands of acres, with the old site of the Fabyan stand, opened in the wilderness, for the travelers' relief, like a desert oasis. Here stand upon the "Giant's Grave," (that famed spot,) where, according to legend, sleeps one of the race which lived in the time of the Saurians and Mastadons! Here lift up your voice, discharge *the shadow of Ethan's cannon, once kept there,* blow a tin horn, or fire a pistol, then listen to the vibration of echo, sounding among a hundred peaks! Ere you bid farewell to the scenery from this mound, behold the westerly declivities of the Titantic brotherhood of craggy White Mountain summits, stretching along the southern sky, with their dark fissures, silvery waterfalls flashing in the sunlight, and deep wide tracks that silently tell where the destroying avalanche has been. Around these mountains are unnumbered streams that afford abundant sport for the trout-catcher.

"The Devil's Den," up the side of Mt. Willard, seen from the notch opposite the *Silver Cascade,* though as yet but imperfectly explored, it deserves a passing notice. From below it appears like a dark hole in the steep cliff, and though various attempts have been made to explore its shadowy secrets, from the day it was first discovered by old Abel Crawford, till 1850 it remained among the unvisited wonders. To F. Leavitt, Esq., belongs the credit of succeeding, by means of a rope let down from the overhanging rock above, in the accomplishment of the daring enterprise of first visiting that spot. Fancy a man suspended over a dark gulf more than a thousand feet deep, by a rope let down from a ragged crag to a dark hole in the mountain, around the entrance of which were scattered the skulls and bones of animals, and you have a glimmering of the picture. Our hero lost all desire to enter that dismal cavern, and kicking the rope, was again drawn up, and since that time, by his description, no explorer has been found with sufficient nerve and curiosity to make a second attempt. As there has never been discovered any possible means by which that den can be approached by foothold up the rock, and as the old *Evil One* has such daily business with mortal affairs, rather than believe that to be his abode, it appears more just to conclude that alone there the mountain eagle finds a solitary home.

BEARING AND DISTANCES OF WHITE MOUNTAINS.

Mount Washington as the centre, from which

Mount	Adams	is distant	4	miles,	N. by E.
"	Jefferson,	"	3	"	N. by W.
"	Madison,	"	5	"	N.N.E.
"	Clay,	"	1	"	N.W.
"	Munroe,	"	1	"	S.W.
"	Franklin,	"	2	"	S.W.
"	Pleasant,	"	3	"	S.W.
"	Clinton,	"	4	"	S.W.

HEIGHT, BEARING AND DISTANCE
OF THE LESS IMPORTANT WHITE MOUNTAINS AND OTHER
MOUNTAINS IN THE VICINITY, FROM MOUNT WASHINGTON.

	Distance		Bearing	Height
Davis Spur,	2	miles	S.S.E.	5,400 feet.
Notch Range,	8	"	S.W.	4,500 "
Willey Mountains,	8	"	S.W.	4,400 "
Mt. Jackson,	6	"	S.W.	4,100 "
Mt. Webster,	7	"	W.N.W.	4,000 "
Giant's Stairs,	8	"	S.	3,500 "
Mt. Crawford,	9	"	S.W.	3,200 "
Mt. Moriah,	7	"	N.E.	4,700 "
Franconia Mount,	20	"	S.W.	5,000 "
Mt. La Fayette,	19	"	W.S.W.	5,200 "
Twin Mountains,	14	"	W.S.W.	4,700, 5,000 "
Mt. Carigain,	14	"	S.S.W.	4,800 "
Moose-hillock,	31	"	S.W.	4,600 "

Saddle Mountain,	22	"	S.S.W.	4,000	"
Mt. Kinsman,	25	"	W.S.W.	4,100	"
Mt. Cannon,	20	"	W.S.W.	4,000	"
Mt. Whiteface,	24	"	S. by W.	4,100	"
Chicorua,	22	"	S. by E.	3,600	"
Kiarsarge,	15	"	S.E.	3,400	"
Double-head,	11	"	S.E.	3,100	"

FRANCONIA AND ITS ATTRACTIONS.

The tourist who would enjoy the whole scenery of this land of mountains and valleys, must not fail to come or go by the way of Franconia. Some of the most prominent attractions of the vicinity, situated 28 miles from the White Mountain Notch, and known by the above poetic title, are the *"Old Man of the Mountains,"* (immortalized by Hawthorne,) *"The Pool," "The Flume," "Franconia Notch," "Mount Lafayette," "Ferrin's Pond,"* (the old man's wash-bowl,) *"The Basin," "The Cascade," "Mt. Cannon,"* and *"Mt. Eagle."*

THE OLD MAN OF THE MOUNTAIN,

is a profile of the human face, situated on a peak of solid rock one thousand feet high, and nearly perpendicular from *"Ferrin's Pond,"* known as the *"old man's washbowl."* This profile was discovered about forty years ago, while a party was laying out the road that passes it, and a guide-board directs the traveler's attention thitherward. This likeness is produced by the irregular projection of five blocks of granite. Its semblance is quite life-like, and is truly a worthy object of wonder. Various Indian utensils and relics have been found in that vicinity, which inclines to the belief that this with the aborigines was an object of superstitious homage. A foot-path from the Lafayette House leads directly over the top of the old man's head, and sometimes a mortal may be seen standing among the bristly hair (bushes) of the old man's foretop. The entire height of this profile is sixty feet.

The Pool is situated midway between the Basin and the Flume. It is about a mile from the Flume House, in a wild, romantic grot, completely walled in by rocky cliffs.

The Flume is about a mile from the main road, and nearly in front of the Flume House. A foot-path through the woods leads the visitor to the spot. A wild mountain torrent, falling over precipitous crags and loose fragments, through high walls, between which hangs a vast granite boulder, under which the water foams.

The Basin is a deep excavation in granite, which has been formed by the wearing waters of the Pemigewasset, aided by the action of stones that the stream has swept into the cavity. In this Basin is a ledge of rock, so worn by the current as to present the form of a leg and foot of giant proportions. This is termed the *"old man's leg."*

The Cascade is below the Flume a short distance. The rock here for the distance of six hundred and twenty feet has been polished by the continual current of the stream to a surface like glass.

Mount Lafayette, or the "great hay-stack," is a lofty conical pile of granite, 5,580 feet high, situated to the south-westward of the village of Franconia. A foot-path leads from the Lafayette House to the top, and the view from that point is considered but little inferior to the prospect from the summit of Mt. Washington.

Mount Eagle, on which is an eagle's eyrie, is fifteen hundred feet high, and rises but a few rods from the Lafayette House. Echo Lake is about two hundred rods from this house, and from its shining waters are taken many of the nicest kinds of trout.

The *Flume House* is, with the *Lafayette House,* well calculated to satisfactorily accommodate all who seek pleasure and health in this mountain region; and taken as a whole, we challenge the territory of our Union to furnish for the Summer tourist a more desirable retreat than our own *White Mountain and Franconia Scenery.*

LENGTH OF DAYS.

The days at the summit of Mt. Washington are about forty minutes longer than on the ocean level, in the same latitude.

THUNDER STORMS

There were but a few thunder storms that approached near to the summit; the greater part of them passing below, and following the deep valley of gulfs, that surround Mt. Washington. But it is a grand sight to behold a black cloud passing along, almost beneath your feet, the lightning playing through it, and the thunder rolling and reverberating among the neighboring mountains, while at the same time the sun is shining brightly upon the tops of the mountains. Yet such scenes are often witnessed, and they fill the mind with awe and wonder.

WHITE MOUNTAIN NAMES FROM OLD RECORD.

As there is a difference of opinion among map and guide makers to these Mountains, in regard to which peak is Mt. Adams, and which is Mt. Jefferson, I have by diligent search obtained the original manuscript, containing the facts which will set all faults in this matter right. In my first edition, and also in this on the twenty-third page, may be found the names of the party which have the honor of first levelling, from below to the top of the different peaks, for the purpose of correctly ascertaining the height of these mountains (the different summits of which had been named the month before). This manuscript was published in J.E. Moore's Historical Collection, in April, 1823, vol. i. page 97. I here make a true extract from the old copy:—

"The White Mountains are situated in the northerly part of the State of New Hampshire, and nearly in the centre of the County of Coos. The latitude of the highest peak is 44° 30 north, or very near it. Every geographical writer in this country, and some beyond the Atlantic, have noticed these mountains; and all agree in assigning to them a greater altitude than to any in New England, if not in the United States. Notwithstanding this acknowledged fact, no two authors agree in assigning to the White Mountains the same height. Had the variation between them been trifling, the public might have rested satisfied, or at least have taken the accounts given by them as correct. But, when they differ in the single circumstance of their altitude more than three thousand feet, the public curiosity, instead of being gratified, is perplexed, and seeks for something approaching to certainly. (Difference in height made by different scientific calculations, see this book on 12th page).

As to the causes of this difference, it is unnecessary to inquire. But it is believed to be out of the power of any person to take the height of mountains correctly, especially such as the White Hills, without using a spirit or water level. This mode is so long, and generally so laborious, that but few persons have had the courage to undertake it. These difficulties notwithstanding, the height of the White Mountains were so taken in August, 1920, by John W. Weeks, Charles J. Stuart, Richard Eastman, and Adino N. Brackett. To accomplish this undertaking they spent seven days, and during five of them were attended by Amos Legro, Joseph W. Brackett, and Edward B. Moore. The whole party were from Lancaster.* The altitude of these mountains above low-water mark in Connecticut River, near the Court House in Lancaster, with the names of the principal peaks, are given below:

Mount Washington rises above the river 5850 feet;** above Austin's (old Whipple place) in Jefferson, 5450 feet; above Crawford's (now Fabyan stand), 4781 feet: this mountain is easily distinguished from the others by its superior elevation (it being the southern of the three highest peaks), and other marks too apparent to need recall. Mount Adams rises above the river 5383 feet, and is known by its sharp terminating peak; Mount Jefferson, 5281 feet, and is situated between the two first. Mount Madison, known by its being the most eastern peak in the range, is above the river 5039 feet. Mount Monroe, the first to the southward of Mount Washington, rises above the river 4932 feet. Mount Franklin, known by its level surface, and being the second southerly of Mount Washington, rises above the

*The party which went up July 31st of the year 1820 have their names recorded back on the 23rd page of this book.

**River here 759 feet above the sea.

river 4470 feet. Mount Pleasant, or Dome Mount, known by its conical shape, and being the third southerly of Mount Washington, rises above the river 4339 feet. Blue Pond (now called "Lakes of the Clouds") lies at the southern base of Mount Washington, and is above the river 4578 feet. This is the description of all the peaks that had up to this date been named; and as the names were given by those who, only one month after, came again, and labored hard for seven days to establish a table that should exhibit correctly the height of each peak according to its name to all coming time, we must conclude that *Mount Adams*, and not Mount Jefferson, is next in height to Mount Washington. On this point Bond's map is wrong, though in all other respects it is the most reliable representation of the localities of the different peaks and points of note connected with White Mountains scenery yet published.

MOUNT WASHINGTON OBSERVATORY

In the spring of 1854, Timothy Estus, of the town of Jefferson, erected upon the summit of Mount Washington a structure, which he called an observatory. It was built 40 feet high, and so arranged that, by means of a rope and gearing, a party of eight could be elevated at a time on a platform 40 feet above the natural top rock, for 50 cents each. This contrivance consisted of four upright posts made of plank bolted together, between which were a great number rods and wooden braces; and from four corners of the main frame-work were extended iron braces, which made the whole capable of withstanding the heaviest storms. This observatory cost about six hundred dollars, and, after being used part of the first season, was abandoned as a total failure. From that time till the summer of 1856 it stood; and the wind howled and whistled and screamed through it, making most unearthly music, till it was that season torn down, and the wood-work was used for firewood.

RAILROAD TO THE TOP OF MT. WASHINGTON

In the June session of 1858, the New Hampshire Legislature granted a charter for a railroad to the top of Mount Washington and to the top of Mount Lafayette, to a man by the name of Sylvester Marsh. That gentleman has the exclusive privilege of controlling the right of constructing such roads, without opposition, any time within twenty years of the date of his charter,—only on to Mount Washington he has no right to lay a track nearer than a fixed distance to any part of the constructed or surveyed route of the new carriage-road from the glen, excepting by consent of the owners of the carriage-road charter (see page 75). The carriage-road here and there spoken of is the one from the glen, that ere this was to have been completed;

but the company that was to have built it has failed, and the road has been located and about half completed, where it now rests, subject to use as a bridle-path, and a splendid monument of a failure. Mr. Marsh has got a model of his engine made, and calculates to gear the speed down to slow motion; and, by means of cog-wheels matched into a middle cog-rail, he expects to run a train of cars up to Tip-Top at a speed of three miles an hour. There was great wonder when the first horse stood on top of Mount Washington; but what will be the expression of the world when the steam-horse puffs his first steam-breath from Tip-Top? The projector calculates the expense of the middle cog-rail at $20,000 a mile.

PLANTS OF THE ALPINE REGIONS
OF THE WHITE MOUNTAINS

Cardamine Bellidifolia, L.; moist places, Great Gulf. Viola Palustris, L.; moist places. Silene Acaulis, L.; rare. Arenaria Groenlandica, Spreng. Alchemilla Alpina, L.; (according to Pursh, but not found since). Sibbaldia Procumbens, L.; (Tuckerman's Ravine; rare. Dryas Integrefolia, Vahl.; (according to Pursh). Geum Peckii, Pursh. Potentilla Minima; Haller. P. Tridentata, L.; Robus Chamoemorus, L.; Mount Clinton. Epilobium Alpinum, L.; moist places. Saxifraga Rivularis, L.; moist places, Great Gulf. Solidago Virga

Aurea, L. Gnaphalium Supinum, Vill.; rare. Arnica Mollis, Hook; moist places. Nabalus Nanus, D.C. N. Boottii, D.C. Campanula Rotundifolia, L.; dwarf alpine state. Vaccinum Vitis Idoea, L. V. Coespitosum, Michx. V. Ulignosum, L.; Arctostaphylos Apina, Spreng.; lower summits. Andromeda Hypnoides, L. Phyllodoce Taxifolia, Salisb. Rhododendron Lapponicum, L. Loiseleuria Decumbens, Desv. Ledum Latifolium, Ait. Veronica Alpina, L. Castilleja Septentrionalis, Lindl. Euphrasia Officinalis, L.; moist places, Oake's Gulf. Rhinanthus Crista Galli, L.; moist places, Oake's Gulf. Diapensia Lapponica, L. Polygonum Viviporum, L.; moist places. Oxyria Digyna, Campd.; moist places, Great Gulf. Empetrum Nigrum, L. Betula Nana, L. Salix Phylicifolia, L.; moist places. S. Uva Ursi; Pursh. S. Repens, L.; moist places. S. Herbacea, L. Luzula Parviflora, Desv. L. Arcuata, Mey. L. Spicata, Desv. Juncus Trifidus, L. Scirpus Coespitosus, L. Eriophorum Alpinum, L. Carex Scirpoidea, Michx. C. Capitata, L. C. Atrata, L. C. Capillaris, L. C. Rigida, Gooden. Phleum Alpinum, L. Argotis Canina, V. Alpina, Oakes. Calamagrostis Sylvatica, D.C. Poa Laxa, Haenk. Festuca Ovina V. Vivipora; moist places, Great Gulf. Aira Atropurpurea, Wahl. Hierochloa Alpina, Roem. and Schult. Lycopodium Selago, L.; L. Annotinum, B. Pungens, Spreng.

There are many other plants of lower regions which

also commonly occur in the alpine; so commonly as to make a list of them proper, which is now necessarily deferred.

Of forest trees, the Balsam Fir (Abies Balsamoea), Marsh; Fraser's Balsam Fir (Abies Fraseri), Pursh; the Yellow Birch (Betula Excelsa, Ait.); and the Paper Birch (Betula Papyracea, Ait.,)—follow the ascent of the mountains, till they disappear in minute shrubs. The Mountain Alder (Alnus Vividus, D.C.) is another very frequent shrub in the higher regions. The Dwarf Raspberry (Rubus Triflorus), Richards; the Swamp Gooseberry (Ribes Lacustre), Poir.; the Skunk Currant (Ribes Prostraum) L'her; the Downy-Leaved Blueberry (Vaccinium Canadense) Kalm.; the common Low Blueberry (Vaccinium Pennsylvanicum) Lam.; and the Small Cranberry (Vaccinium Oxycoccus) L.;—are common fruits of the alpine solitudes. The two species of Streptopus; Veratrum Vivide, Ait.; Kalmia Glauca, Ait.; Linnae Borealis, Gronov.; Cornus Canadensis, L.; Thalictrum Cornuti, L.; Aster Acuminatus, Michx.; Solidago Thrysoidea, Mey.; Houstonic Coerulea, L.; Coptis Trifolia, Salisb.; Claytonia Virginica, L.; Stellaria Borealis, Bigel.,—will all occur to the botanist. A dwarf state of Eriophorum Vaginatum, L.; Carex Limosa, L.; C. Irrigua, Sm.; C. Caneseens, in the more alpine variety, B.; Alpicola, Wahl., in the higher regions, and the taller greener state; Sphoerostachya, Tuckerm., in the lower,—are among the Cyperacea. And Avena Striata, Michx., and Hierochloa Borealis, Roem. and Schult., interesting grapes. And the most elevated mountain lakes which have any (other than crytogamic) vegetation, are adorned by Nuphar Advena, Ait., and a species of Sparganium, with long floating leaves, which the late Mr. Oakes regarded distinct. This is to be taken for only a rough sketch of the botany of the highest parts of the White Mountains.

REMARKABLE FEATS IN WHITE-MOUNTAIN LIFE

A.S. Walker of Boston, walked up from the Glen to the top of Mount Washington, bare-footed, July 27, 1855.

George N. Dana, Boston, counted his steps from the Glen to the top of Mount Washington, August 2, 1857. Number of steps, 16,925.

John Irving, of New York, walked up on time from the Glen to the top of Mount Washington, August, 1855, in an hour and fifty-seven minutes.

Miss Cune, of Boston, walked from the Glen up through Tuckerman's Ravine, to the top of Mount Washington, without a guide, August 26, 1856. She was dressed like a Swiss peasant, and wore the same shoes, and carried the same steel-pointed staff, that she used the year before in crossing the Alps.

A Miss Prentiss, of Paris, Me., walked up from the

Glen, August 22, 1856, without a guide, in a snow-storm, to the top of Mount Washington.

The 25th of July, 1855, a lady by the name of Branch walked from the Glen to Tip-Top and back, the same day, on a bet of one thousand dollars. She accomplished the feat, and danced at the Glen in the evening. The cause of the bet was on account of her weight being 230 lbs. She was of medium height, and the heaviest lady that ever visited Tip-Top.

Nathaniel Perkins, of Jefferson, run from the top of Mount Washington down on the Glen path,—one mile,—on a bet of sixty dollars. He bet that sum that he could accomplish that feat in eight minutes; and he performed in it six minutes and fifty-seven seconds. This was in August, 1853.

A gentleman from New York city walked from the Crawford House up to the top of Mount Washington, after eleven o'clock at night, and arrived on Tip-Top at three in the morning. This was in 1855.

HEIGHT OF THE DIFFERENT MOUNTAIN HOUSES ABOVE THE SEAS

Tip-Top House, Mount Washington, ...	6,285 feet
Crawford House, ...	1,919 "
Glen House, ...	1,615 "
Ruins of Fabyan's House, ...	1,576 "
Brabrook House, ...	1,568 "
Davis House, ...	978 "
Alpine House, ...	802 "

Distances of the other Mountain Homes from the Tip-Top House on Mount Washington:—

Alpine House,	15 miles; 8 by stage; 7, ponies
Brabrook,	10 "	7 "	3, "
Fabyan,	9 "	6 "	3, "
Crawford,	9 "		"
Glen,	7 "		"

FREIGHT OF BUILDING MATERIALS TO TIP-TOP

The building materials of the Summit House were brought up from the Glen side (excepting the stones); and those of the Tip-Top House were brought up from the northerly side, towards Randolph. The boards were fastened upon the sides of horses by small chains. The longest timbers, which are twenty-eight feet long, and weighed when green four hundred, were brought up from four miles below, two at a time,—hitched by one end on to the side of a pack-saddle, and the other was allowed to drag. The stores were brought up in pieces, packed in leather bags; and the chairs and beds, carpets, doors, and dishes, tables, &c., were all brought up on horses' backs. The Tip-Top and Summit Houses costs seven thousand dollars.

DEATH OF LIZZIE BOURNE.

Down on the Glen path, forty rods from the top of Mt. Washington, stands a little monument of stone. There, on the morning of September 14th, 1855, the body of Lizzie Bourne, daughter of E.E. Bourne, Esq., of Kennebunk, Me., was found. About two o'clock the day before, she had started from the Glen House, accompanied by her uncle, George W. Bourne, and his daughter, to walk to the top of Mount Washington. Sunshine was around their steps as they walked cheerfully up the new carriage road, but on gaining the "Bald Ledge," they became enveloped in a dense black cloud that had all day been hanging on Mt. Washington. Still their courage was good, and they hastened on against the strong wind until within nineteen rods of the Summit House, where, drenched by the wildly flying mists, and having lost her bonnet, poor Lizzie sat down and complained of being sleepy. Well knowing that inaction would be certain death thus exposed, and finding Lizzie unable to climb higher, the uncle, with the aid of his daughter, thought to lead her back a short distance, in hopes she might revive and be able to turn and go up. She fell down in the path where the mound now stands; and when sure that she had breathed her last, the uncle laid around her a pile of stones to break the rude blasts of the wind, and with his daughter sought shelter for the remainder of that dismal night under a ledge now to be seen some six or eight steps above where her body was found, on the same side of the path. She was about 22 years of age, and doubtless her death was occasioned by some disease of the heart, hastened by exertion. Her mother and an only sister had both died of disease of the heart. Poor Lizzie was carried down the mountain on a rude bier by four stout mountaineers.

ADVENTURE OF DR. B. L. BALL
ON MT. WASHINGTON.

The 24th of October, 1855, Dr. Ball left the Glen House to walk up the new carriage road as far as *"The Ledge,"* where some workmen were then camping. Previous to starting, he had decided to go to the summit of Mt. Washington, though the snow was, as he afterwards found, about a foot deep, and the Tip-Top House was shut up for the season. The first evening he walked past the camp to the Ledge, and having climbed up to the Bald Rock, he became enveloped in clouds, and the snow being deep, and darkness coming on, he hastened back to the camp, and by the kindness of Mr. Myers was made comfortable through the night. Next morning, after taking a bowl of coffee and a few mouthfuls of food, he started again to go up to the summit. The snow had in part disappeared during the night, but the mountain was still covered with clouds, and, guided by the line of stakes that mark the route for the new carriage road, he proceeded up to where the snow became deeper, and having lost his way, wandered till night. As it became dark he retreated down the mountain, to a bunch of scrub trees, and with his umbrella for a shelter, passed a sleepless night, without fire, and with ice upon his clothing, his hands and feet frozen; and even after this, he was thoroughly chilled by the high wind, and compelled to wander thirty-six hours longer, without food, rest, or shelter; and at last was only barely rescued from the embrace of death by the untiring exertions of six hardy mountaineers, who, on learning that a gentleman was lost, started in search. J.S. Hall was the first to discover the object of their search. Much surprise was manifested at finding him yet alive, as he had been over sixty hours exposed to extreme cold, without food, without rest, and with nothing but snow and ice to quench his thirst. This is the most remarkable record of great exposure in this mountain region to be found on any page of White Mountain life.

THE FATE OF BENJAMIN CHANDLER.

The 4th of August, 1856, Benjamin Chandler left the city of Wilmington, Del., with the intention of visiting the New England States. He arrived at the Glen House August 7th, and late in the afternoon of that day, with a little bundle under his arm, started to walk alone to the top of Mt. Washington. That day on Tip-Top was rainy, and that evening clouds were hurled wildly over the dripping rocks by a cold northeast wind. At

dark, or a little after, two ministers, the Rev. S.J.
Spaulding, of Newburyport, Mass., and Rev. Charles
Smith, of Boston, arrived at the Tip-Top House, saying, as they sat down, dripping wet, "We passed an old
gentleman half way down, and he will hardly get up
along to-night." After making certain inquiries, a guide
was started out from the Tip-Top House, with a lan-
tern, who, after going down nearly a mile, lost his light
by the high wind, and after shouting many times as loud
as he could in vain, he returned wet and cold, where-
upon the proprietor of Tip-Top concluded that the old
gentleman must have stopped for the night with some
road workmen who were camping at the "Ledge." Next
morning search was made, but as no information could
be obtained, the general conclusion was the old man
might have turned back and left the mountain. All remained a mystery till, late in September, David Chandler, son of the missing man, came in search. July 19th,
1857, Ambrose Tower, of New York, came across a
skeleton about half a mile eastward from the top of
Mt. Washington. A gold watch, $57 in bills, $52 in
gold, and a few dollars in silver, with a pair of spec-
tacles, a pocket knife, railroad ticket, &c., were found
upon his person. No doubt remains in the minds of the
witnesses about this being the skeleton of Benjamin
Chandler. Report says he was about seventy-five years
of age, had been for about fifty years connected with

the Masonic fraternity, and had held for a long time the highest rank known to the Order in this country. Since his loss, the appraisal of his property fixes the amount at one hundred thousand dollars. He was a man of very active habits, had a great inclination to ask questions, and had at times been deranged.

THERMOMETRICAL TABLE,

And Synopsis Of The Weather, &C., &C., At The Summit Of Mt. Washington,
For The Seasons Of 1853-1857.

JUNE, 1853.   JULY, 1853.

Day.	Sunrise.	12M.	Sunset.	Day.	Sunrise.	12M.	Sunset.
8	32	40	34	1	43	55	45
9	31	45	40	2	32	46	38
10	38	52	48	3	44	53	48
11	44	47	43	4	52	60	54
12	32	48	44	5	42	51	42
13	43	56	47	6	39	48	39
14	48	60	55	7	29	47	37
15	53	59	55	8	38	50	49
16	54	62	55	9	41	49	45
17	54	56	52	10	45	50	45
18	43	48	40	11	45	54	48
19	39	49	42	12	40	52	45
20	50	66	58	13	38	49	45
21	48	57	50	14	42	59	49
22	54	58	55	15	52	62	51
23	58	60	55	16	51	56	52
24	56	42	35	17	44	49	37
25	30	36	32	18	39	55	48
26	24	37	30	19	52	53	50
27	32	44	38	20	42	50	41
28	34	43	35	21	38	45	46
29	45	64	58	22	42	60	56
30	54	61	53	23	50	66	56
				24	54	64	59
				25	52	63	55
				26	50	51	45
				27	43	59	54
				28	39	47	45
				29	44	59	54
				30	49	59	56
				31	50	59	49

AUGUST, 1853.   SEPTEMBER, 1853.

Day.	Sunrise.	12M.	Sunset.	Day.	Sunrise.	12M.	Sunset.
1	42	59	50	1	41	51	47
2	49	51	49	2	45	58	55
3	48	58	49	3	50	58	55
4	49	54	48	4	52	55	54
5	45	54	53	5	50	58	57
6	51	60	49	6	57	59	56
7	46	53	48	7	56	49	45
8	49	58	48	8	30	40	36
9	50	52	52	9	33	44	41
10	48	59	57	10	37	40	32
11	52	62	59	11	28	29	27
12	52	60	59	12	24	29	30
13	59	60	59	13	32	36	39
13	59	60	56	14	38	46	42
14	58	60	50	15	45	50	47
15	45	57	53	16	38	42	
16	50	56	55				
17	49	62	55				
18	48	58	51				
19	33	37	33				
20	30	35	36				
21	36	46	45				
22	39	40	35				
23	33	43	42				
24	37	46	45				
25	44	42	36				
26	31	47	42				
27	42	47	47				
28	34	35	32				
29	31	46	43				
30	38	51	50				
31	46	49	46				

JUNE 1854.

Day.	Sunrise.	12 M.	Sunset.	Self-Register during Night
10	44	46	40	36
11	38	46	45	38
12	42	52	47	42
13	48	58	48	44
14	46	54	45	45
15	46	52	46	41
16	42	46	36	29
17	31	41	42	42
18	48	54	51	48
19	49	54	52	46
20	46	51	42	40
21	43	57	50	45
22	50	57	50	45
23	46	49	48	44
24	44	48	46	39
25	39	44	36	33
26	34	48	44	36
27	42	52	47	46
28	54	58	56	36
29	36	54	48	42
30	46	46	46	40

JULY, 1854.

Day.	Sunrise.	12 M.	Sunset.	Self-Register during Night
1	40	42	42	39
2	40	48	48	48
3	54	58	58	53
4	54	60	60	54
5	54	54	50	40
6	40	48	46	46
7	49	56	58	50
8	50	57	56	56
9	60	60	54	45
10	45	50	48	40
11	40	56	56	45
12	46	54	46	31
13	32	51	47	44
14	44	58	51	50
15	50	62	54	50
16	50	64	58	53
17	54	62	57	46
18	48	50	55	55
19	55	63	61	55
20	56	70	63	57
21	58	60	58	51
22	52	62	58	52
23	54	55	57	51
24	53	56	54	54
25	54	60	55	54
26	56	60	54	39
27	39	45	40	38
28	41	50	49	45
29	48	49	52	45
30	47	48	44	40
31	40	50	51	48

AUGUST, 1854.   SEPTEMBER, 1854.

Day.	Sunrise.	12 M.	Sunset.	Self-Register during Night	Day.	Sunrise.	12 M.	Sunset.	Self-Register during Night
1	50	61	56	52	1	48	52	50	
2	54	51	46	36	2	38	50	50	
3	38	40	45	44	3	51	52	51	
4	46	47	46	43	4	40	50	49	
5	45	56	54	47	5	54	60	59	
6	47	54	45	31	6	58	64	57	
7	33	38	36	32	7	52	49	42	
8	33	42	38	32	8	33	41	45	
9	34	66	48	36	9	46	45	43	
10	38	56	50	44	10	32	42	34	
11	45	60	54	49	11	32	46	46	
12	49	52	52	51	12	40	48	46	
13	52	54	51	33	13	30	40	45	
14	33	34	36	32	14	36	42	38	
15	41	47	45	44	15	40	40	32	
16	48	55	49	48	16	36			
17	48	55	48	46					
18	47	50	40	39					
19	39	58	48	44					
20	45	59	50	46					
21	46	50	48	40					
22	42	49	40	30					
23	30	54	52	50					
24	50	56	50	36					
25	36	40	38	38					
26	39	44	46	45					
27	46	44	38	39					
28	39	48	43	39					
29	39	56	60	48					
30	48	50	57	51					
31	51	56	60	48					

JUNE, 1855.

Day.	Sunrise.	12M.	Sunset.
20	50	55	48
21	47	60	50
22	54	58	54
23	58	57	48
24	30	44	50
25	44	50	50
26	54	60	48
27	50	58	50
28	52	48	44
29	36	40	40
30	34	41	40

JULY, 1855.

Day.	Sunrise.	12M.	Sunset.
1	43	53	40
2	33	40	38
3	45	50	41
4	50	60	50
5	40	55	48
6	32	40	35
7	39	36	32
8	36	42	40
9	40	55	50
10	45	50	44
11	48	56	50
12	50	60	55
13	50	54	51
14	44	50	42
15	49	54	51
16	51	58	50
17	43	60	44
18	39	50	42
19	42	52	40
20	50	61	45
21	44	52	36
22	46	48	51
23	40	51	40
24	50	54	52
25	50	52	52
26	48	63	55
27	50	60	56
28	46	57	60
29	50	56	53
30	50	58	54
31	50	54	53

AUGUST, 1855.   SEPTEMBER, 1855.

Day.	Sunrise.	12M.	Sunset.	Day.	Sunrise.	12M.	Sunset.
1	45	58	52	1	45	56	54
2	45	59	53	2	48	55	44
3	46	57	52	3	29	48	40
4	52	53	46	4	31	46	39
5	42	52	45	5	30	45	40
6	41	46	38	6	35	52	46
7	35	37	36	7	38	50	44
8	30	50	38	8	46	46	52
9	43	52	50	9	54	53	46
10	40	40	38	10	37	46	44
11	31	55	40	11	40	46	44
12	38	57	50	12	53	55	56
13	50	50	47	13	54	40	35
14	34	44	37	14	29	39	42
15	33	47	45	15	33	44	38
16	48	45	48	16	40	46	44
17	50	51	40	17	43	47	45
18	26	28	30	18	38	40	26
19	28	31	34	19	14	17	
20	30	44	40				
21	42	53	41				
22	44	60	48				
23	52	52	48				
24	44	50	46				
25	38	48	48				
26	44	50	48				
27	38	42	39				
28	32	40	38				
29	32	52	44				
30	28	26	24				
31	20	24	26				

JUNE, 1856.

Day.	Sunrise.	12M.	Sunset.
17		44	45
18	40	43	46
19	38	42	47
20	42	46	44
21	43	45	45
22	44	45	44
23	42	46	43
24	32	52	39
25	38	48	48
26	40	50	43
27	37	39	35
28	32	40	33
29	31	62	60
30	51	56	51

JULY, 1856.

Day.	Sunrise.	12M.	Sunset.
1	30	32	39
2	31	42	45
3	41	51	37
4	42	39	41
5	31	48	33
6	40	47	44
7	30	45	45
8	43	51	42
9	43	48	42
10	42	46	43
11	44	57	50
12	47	50	50
13	52	57	54
14	45	50	50
15	50	49	46
16	40	50	52
17	49	55	57
18	54	60	50
19	36	39	39
20	38	38	36
21	36	46	42
22	38	46	44
23	42	52	52
24	48	57	54
25	50	58	55
26	50	60	56
27	54	60	53
28	50	52	54
29	52	53	52
30	51	60	54
31	53	62	54

AUGUST, 1856.   SEPTEMBER, 1856.

Day.	Sunrise.	12M.	Sunset.	Day.	Sunrise.	12M.	Sunset.
1	54	62	55	1	18	37	36
2	55	63	57	2	30	48	46
3	50	66	54	3	34	50	46
4	50	66	56	4	38	48	43
5	50	60	51	5	44	58	54
6	50	54	52	6	38	54	52
7	53	52	45	7	44	56	49
8	43	53	50	8	44	46	42
9	45	54	50	9	38	42	42
10	42	54	42	10	44	54	52
11	42	56	47	11	52	53	40
12	38	58	41	12	28	36	38
13	38	39	40	13	38	40	
14	38	43	42				
15	38	42	40				
16	39	41	40				
17	40	46	45				
18	42	50	40				
19	39	45	39				
20	39	40	35				
21	33	34	33				
22	32	35	37				
23	39	43	41				
24	42	42	36				
25	35	32	28				
26	22	23	24				
27	28	30	32				
28	32	42	42				
29	40	44	43				
30	30	33	32				
31	29	33	30				

The coldest indicated by our self registering thermometer, in the winters of 1856-7, was 40° below zero. The thermometer was left hung to a beam of the barroom of the Tip-Top House.

In the summer of 1856, June 29 and July 7, there was ice on Tip-Top; and, the 27th day of August of that year, there fell on Mount Washington two inches of snow.

JUNE, 1857.   JULY, 1857.

Day.	Sunrise.	12M.	Sunset.	Day.	Sunrise.	12M.	Sunset.
20		50	45	1	28	34	33
21	42	42	43	2	29	44	36
22	40	45	44	3	34	48	42
23	33	32	31	4	37	48	40
24	26	32	35	5	38	58	47
25	32	40	38	6	40	54	50
26	35	39	37	7	46	45	40
27	34	42	40	8	28	35	34
28	37	50	46	9	34	45	41
29	37	56	47	10	41	56	46
30	37	52	36	11	46	58	51
				12	50	60	54
				13	52	58	52
				14	52	60	57
				15	51	65	58
				16	51	69	56
				17	47	66	48
				18	47	57	50
				19	50	64	52
				20	48	57	50
				21	47	60	52
				22	47	61	56
				23	46	46	44
				24	46	56	48
				25	50	52	48
				26	46	51	50
				27	50	60	52
				28	53	58	50
				29	42	40	38
				30	38	58	50
				31	39	54	46

AUGUST, 1857.   SEPTEMBER, 1857.

Day.	Sunrise.	12M.	Sunset.	Day.	Sunrise.	12M.	Sunset.
1	41	56	49	1	38	49	46
2	36	50	39	2	48	58	52
3	48	52	51	3	45	52	46
4	51	60	52	4	43	66	50
5	48	56	51	5	43	50	46
6	44	52	52	6	28	28	25
7	47	60	54	7	20	25	20
8	51	53	44	8	18	30	30
9	42	58	54	9	31	36	36
10	46	58	53	10	40	44	47
11	42	48	50	11	48	50	50
12	38	42	44	12	46	46	48
13	48	52	48	13	44	48	47
14	53	53	50	14	44	50	50
15	40	40	40	15	40	32	30
16	25	30	33	16	19	26	20
17	31	40	40	17	24	34	34
18	34	40	34	18	16	30	30
19	28	52	44				
20	37	40	40				
21	37	42	40				
22	34	50	44				
23	35	50	46				
24	39	42	39				
25	26	40	40				
26	37	46	48				
27	38	50	48				
28	39	50	49				
29	42	46	48				
30	36	32	30				
31	32	37	36				

Our self-registering thermometer indicated, as the coldest for the winter 1857-58, 35° below zero.

In the summer of 1857, in the mornings of June 24, July 1, and August 16 and 25, and September 6, 8, 16, and 18, the top of Mount Washington was covered with a thick coat of new ice.